Italian Cooking From Scratch

How to Make Fresh Homemade Pasta, Grow Your Own Herbs and Vegetables and Cook Classical Italian Recipes

Eric Beuning

CONTENTS

Foreword

By Stephen McDonald (Publisher)

The combination of these three short books creates an intimate overview of the process of cooking great Italian food, from garden to table. The first is an indispensable quick start guide to the inspiring process of cooking pasta from scratch. The second and third are cookbooks about gardening and gardening books about cooking.

Each of these three books is about connecting with the important ways in which food can enhance our lives, making our experience with food rich, satisfying and more deeply connected. It is about honoring the ingredients in our food and embracing the processes we use in preparing them. I hope you enjoy the wisdom and the recipes in this collection as much as I have.

Part I - Understanding Italian Pasta and Sauce

Making Pasta from Scratch and Cooking Classical Italian Pasta Dishes

(a short recipe guide and unconventional cookbook)

Introduction

When most people think of Italian cooking they think of pasta. Sitting down at an Italian restaurant to eat a big steaming bowl of pasta soaked in a rich marinara or cheese sauce has become a classic American comfort food.

It's very tempting to want to make the same pasta dishes at home. People who take that first step often start at the grocery store looking at a box of dried pasta and a jar of thin, over salted sauce. Following the recipe on the side of the jar usually falls short of expectations. At the same time, for the average American home cook the idea of making pasta and sauce from scratch can feel like a tall mountain to climb.

These days the knee jerk reaction is to turn to the internet for help. Unfortunately, what you usually find with an internet search is an ingredient list and instructions that are an eloquent way of saying "Just dump everything together and stir." To really honor a dish and understand the process you need to get your hands on it and build some authentic experience.

In some of my other books I tell the story of how I grew up at the apron strings of my adopted Italian Grandma. She was born in Naples Italy and immigrated to America after World War Two where she ran an Italian Restaurant. She and her husband retired just a few weeks before I was born and agreed to take care of me while my Mother worked double shifts. I called them Grandma and Papa.

I grew up eating classic Italian dishes as well as new American tweaks on the Italian food that was so popular in American restaurants through the 60's 70's and 80's. After Grandma and Papa died I dedicated myself to learning how to recreate the classical Italian dishes of my childhood. Some people think of their childhood favorites and Grandma's cooking as being chicken noodle soup and fresh baked cookies. I think of spaghetti Bolognese and cheese stuffed ravioli.

It was a long process to learn how to make these dishes. A lot of Italian cooking is about learning to take a simple quality ingredient and honor it by treating it right. There are some common mistakes that can ruin a dish and little tweaks that can make it shine.

In the coming chapters we'll take a look at how to decide between cooking with dried pasta or fresh pasta; including the procedures for making your own fresh pasta. We'll also look at how to make classic Italian sauces paired with classic pasta dishes. There are sure to be some twists and turns along the way.

This isn't a compendium of all Italian Pasta recipes. With all the decorative pastas out there in the world, and all the regional variations you can apply to them, the subject is too vast to be put into one short book. Instead think of this as a guide to help you get your feet wet. This book will help you get some authentic experience under your belt so you can figure out where you want to go next in your great Italian cooking adventure!

Chapter 1 – Making Fresh Pasta

A Note about Dried Pasta

The dried pasta you find in your local grocery store is usually made in a factory. They use a large amount of semolina flour in the pasta recipe. Then they dry it in a process that slowly adjusts the specific humidity. The end result is hard pasta that has a long shelf life but only a small amount of flavor.

The biggest problem when cooking dried pasta is the fact that the noodles are not very absorbent. Most good Italian pasta dishes call for you to finish cooking the pasta in the sauce. This allows it to bind the sauce to the pasta enhancing its ability to be a vehicle for flavor.

As a result, dry pasta is best when paired with oily rich sauces or applications like Carbonara where the heat of the pasta is what is finishing the cooking of the sauce.

Don't get me wrong, I'm not trying to put down all dry pastas everywhere. In fact most decorative pastas like farfalle (also known as bow ties) are dried pastas. Because of the tedious nature involved in making decorative pasta, it is hard to make them from fresh pasta and expect the first noodle to have the same texture as the last.

Convenience is the biggest factor to consider with dried pasta. I have made macaroni from scratch and the process was painstakingly tedious. The sheer time and labor of making the macaroni threw off the timing of everything else I was cooking. The end result was an under whelming plate of pasta and a nasty neck ache. I would honestly rather fall down a flight of steps on my face than make macaroni from scratch ever again!

Fresh Pasta

While there are times when dried pasta is called for, it still remains a principled truth that fresh pasta is the best choice for most classic Italian dishes.

When walking through the refrigerator case of the grocery store, you might see one of those clear plastic cases of pasta that is labeled as being “Fresh” and be tempted to grab it. The reality is these shouldn’t be called fresh pasta. It’s just that “Premade soft pasta product” doesn’t exactly roll off the tongue.

Most of the time, these prepackaged versions are made with dough stabilizers and other additives to help them keep longer in grocery store cases. Many of these additives keep the pasta from interacting with the sauce. The pasta tends to slide around in the sauce like two strangers instead of forming a harmonious relationship with it.

The price for these packages of premade pasta is usually very high when compared to the cheap price of rolling out fresh pasta made from flour and eggs at home.

Fresh pasta made at home and often finished in the sauce has the ability to form a relationship with the sauce in a way that benefits both components. The process is actually rather easy once you understand the principles of making and rolling it out. All at the cost of around a dollar!

A quick tour of a pasta roller

Growing up in Grandma's kitchen I never once saw a pasta roller machine. Grandma always used a French rolling pin and a floured cutting board to roll out the dough. Then she used a razor sharp meat cleaver much the way most people today use a chef's knife.

If you have burly forearms, steady nerves and the patience of my Italian Grandma, you can indeed make fresh pasta this way. I did it this way for years. It wasn't until I got married and my wife informed me that I was absolutely crazy that the notion of using a pasta roller or stand mixer attachment came into play.

If you own a stand mixer then you're probably aware of the giant cloud of random attachments available for it. To be honest with you I've only ever seen one pasta roller attachment for a stand mixer that I thought was worth anything. It cost $80 and still was inferior to a $50 hand crank model.

Since my wife has dragged me kicking and screaming into the 21st century I can admit to loving the hand crank pasta roller. The hand crank model allows you to control the speed at which you send the tender pasta dough through the roller.

This is absolutely critical when you find a tear starting to form. You just can't get this with a stand mixer attachment unless you use your mixer daily and have an intimate feel for the variable speed control.

A hand crank pasta roller is ultimately a pretty simple device. It is usually made from stainless steel or aluminum. The crank turns the rollers and a dial on the side allows you to control the distance between those rollers.

Most rollers have 6 to 7 thickness settings. Settings 6 and 5 are for folding, binding or preparing pasta dough to handle thinner settings. You will actually run pasta through these settings and fold the ends back into the middle, in order to strengthen the pasta for the thinner settings. If you try to bypass these thick settings and folding procedures the dough tends to rip apart during the crucial thin rolling.

The top two or three settings are essentially there to fold and bind the dough together. While there are some noodles, such as a thick fettuccine, that can use the number 5 setting, you will rarely use it.

Setting 4 and 3 are the most common thicknesses for pasta. This is the thickness for your sheets of lasagna, strands of linguine and folds of ravioli. When you go below setting 2 you are moving into the world of delicate pasta like angel hair. The tenderness of pasta at these settings calls for absolute care and you want to turn the crank at a speed slightly faster than continental drift!

Fresh Pasta Recipe

To a purist pasta is nothing more than eggs and all-purpose flour. You make a mound of flour with a dent in the middle big enough to nest three eggs into it. Break the yolks with a fork or your fingers and stir to combine. The eggs will absorb as much of the flour as possible and you'll have a dough ball that needs to be kneaded.

There are a lot of different permutations and additions you can make to this recipe. Some people add minced garlic; others add herbs or even black pepper. There are even variations out there that add pureed winter squash to the eggs or instant potatoes to the flour.

Over the years the years I've played with the recipe tweaking a little bit to my tastes and texture preference. I include a little semolina flour to the mixture. Semolina flour can usually be found in the organic section or the baking aisle of your local grocery store. Semolina is made from durum wheat, which has higher protein content.

Adding a little semolina improves the texture and durability of the pasta. However, too much semolina will reduce the pasta's ability to absorb the sauce in some applications. So if you are going to deviate from my tweaked recipe, be mindful of how this will affect the pasta's relationship to the sauce of your choice.

I also like to add just a little olive oil and salt to punch up the flavors, they are certainly optional. I'm sure there are some pasta purists, who cook regional Italian variations, who would argue that my recipe would not be considered authentic pasta. If you want to take the purist view of the recipe, simply use only 3 large eggs and 2 cups of all-purpose flour.

The following is a recipe for creating a sheet of fresh pasta. In the recipes section later in the book we'll look at the different types of pasta and how the sheet of pasta should be cut or used to suit each recipe.

Equipment

A pasta roller

A floured cutting board

Plastic wrap

Board scraper

Ingredients

2 Cups of all-purpose flour

½ Cup semolina flour

½ Teaspoon salt

1 Tablespoon of olive oil

3 Large eggs

1 Egg Yolk

Procedure

Step 1: On a floured cutting board combine the two types of flour and form into a mound with a depression in the middle large enough to hold the eggs.

Step 2: Carefully crack the eggs, separate one additional yolk and add them to the nest made by the pasta. Break each yolk with a fork or your fingertips.

Step 3: Add the olive oil and begin working the mixture together with your fingertips. The water content of the egg will only absorb so much flour and the dough will tell you when it has come together. There should be a little bit of flour leftover on the board when you are done. If the dough is sticky at all dust with a little more flour.

Step 4: Once the dough has come together let it rest on the counter for 5 minutes. This resting period will allow the water content of the eggs to completely saturate and hydrate the flour. When flour is properly saturated it allows for more gluten formation. Gluten gives the pasta its structure and strength. Salt also interferes with the hydration process which is why it has been withheld so far.

Step 5: Sprinkle the salt evenly over the dough then fold it in half from east to west. Fold in half from north to south. Continue kneading in this way until the dough comes together into a firm ball.

If, in the course of kneading, the dough is clearly too dry and breaks apart, wet your hands with tap water and caress the dough ball with your wet hands. Wait 1 minute and begin kneading the damp dough in.

Once the salt has been incorporated and the dough holds a ball shape, knead for 5 minutes like you would bread dough.

Step 6: Wrap the dough ball tightly with plastic wrap and place it in the refrigerator for a half hour. This resting time will allow the dough to completely hydrate and the firm up the gluten chains that were formed during kneading.

Step 7: Secure the pasta roller to the counter and lightly flour the work station for 16 inches beyond the bottom of the roller. This way when you make your final long sheets they will stretch out on the floured surface instead of sticking to the counter.

Step 8: Remove the dough ball from the plastic wrap. Using a board scraper cut the dough ball into quarters. Work each quarter into a rectangle

Step 9: Set the pasta roller on its thickest setting. Roll the rectangle through the pasta roller. When it comes out fold both ends into the middle and press it together. Run it through the pasta maker on the widest setting again. Fold both ends into the middle again. By folding and rolling this way you create a more durable noodle that will resist tearing as you continue to roll it thinner and thinner.

Step 10: Set the pasta roller one step thinner and run it through.

Step 11: Continue setting the pasta roller one step thinner until you have reached the desired thickness. For most pasta types this is a thickness setting of 3 or 4.

If you are looking for cut noodles such as linguine or fettuccine, follow the instructions on the pasta cutter attachment. Or you can flour the sheet, roll it loosely and cut it to the desired width with a sharp chef's knife.

Cutting a rolled sheet of pasta with a knife is a bit of an art form. Too much pressure when rolling can cause the layers to stick. Cutting with a dull knife or using too much of a sawing motion can cause the cut edges to bind and will look sloppy when you separate them.

Cutting with a knife is something that really does take a lot of practice. So it is best to learn the specific procedures of the pasta cutter attachment that comes with your roller machine.

Chapter 2 –Making Classic Marinara Sauce

The coming chapters will feature classic pasta and sauce combinations. They are not hard and fast rules to cook by. Merely they are classic pairings that do the best job of demonstrating the strengths of both pasta and sauce. In many cases you can change them up. If you want to pair fettuccine with Bolognese sauce instead of spaghetti there certainly is nothing wrong with that. However it might not be the best idea to use a carbonara sauce with ravioli as the surface area of the pasta might not cook the sauce through.

My suggestion, before you start getting creative with pasta and sauce pairings, is to create each classic original recipe the first time just to understand it. Once you've got a grasp of the relationship between the sauce and the pasta the creative options really open up from there. Let's do some cooking.

Classic Marinara Sauce Recipe

This is a general purpose marinara sauce. It can stand alone being tossed with many types of pasta. You can also make additions to it so that it can pair up with other unique pasta dishes. For instance when making meat lasagna you would add browned Italian sausage and mushrooms along with green peppers.

Equipment

Medium sauce pot

Ladle

Ingredients

2 Pounds of diced plum tomatoes (such as Roma)

1 Large yellow onion, chopped

4 Cloves of garlic, minced

8 Leaves of fresh basil, chopped

3 Tablespoons fresh oregano, chopped

Pinch salt

Pinch fresh ground black pepper

Pinch sugar

¼ Cup olive oil

Procedure

Step 1: Add olive oil to a medium sauce pot over a medium high heat. Allow a few minutes for the oil to come up to temp.

Step 2: Add the onions and sauté until they start becoming translucent. Add the garlic and sauté for one minute until golden.

Step 3: Add the tomatoes. Stir to combine and bring to a simmer.

Step 4: Add the basil, oregano, salt and pepper. Simmer on a low heat, stirring occasionally for 15 minutes.

Step 5: Taste the sauce, if it seems a bit green or bitter, add a pinch of sugar.

Chapter 3 –Lasagna

Lasagna is a classic Italian dish that has found a new home as an American comfort food. Traditionally it is made from sheets of pasta layered with marinara sauce and cheese. Lasagna's popularity in America has spawned many different variations. Vegetables, chicken, cheese and beef are used in many combinations across the country.

A lot of recipes call for the use of dried pasta sold in fluted or wavy sheets. Some recipes call for boiling the noodles first, others talk about the glory of using a no-boil technique. To be honest with you I'm sure my Italian Grandma would rise from the grave and poke a sharp stick in my eye if I used anything other than fresh pasta to make this dish.

For the sheets you will want to make one and a half pounds of fresh pasta. You should roll out enough for the bottom layer that it covers a 13X9 baking pan at a number 4 thickness. All the rest of the pasta layers should be at a number 3 thickness.

Normally I make lasagna with vegetables straight from the garden and the freshest mozzarella I can find. I've made some tweaks to this recipe to make it a little easier to find what you need at the average American grocery store. This recipe is for classic meat lasagna, after making it once you should be able to make any other creative changes.

Equipment

13 X 9 deep baking dish or lasagna pan

Large sauce pan

Ladle

Medium sized work bowl

Ingredients for cheese layer

1 Pound container of ricotta cheese

1 Pound of mozzarella cheese, grated

1 Pound of sliced mozzarella cheese

½ Cup of parmesan cheese

1 Large egg

6 Cloves of garlic, minced

½ Red onion, chopped fine

¼ Cup of fresh parsley, chopped

1/4 Cup fresh basil, chopped

1 Tablespoon fresh oregano, chopped

1 Teaspoon sea salt

1 Teaspoon fresh cracked black pepper

Procedure for cheese layer

A half hour before you start the meat sauce, combine all ingredients except the sliced mozzarella and one half pound of the grated mozzarella. Stir thoroughly to combine and let rest in the refrigerator to allow flavors to meld.

Ingredients for meat sauce

2 Large cans of diced tomatoes

1 Large yellow onion, chopped

1 Pound of Mushrooms, sliced

1 Pound Italian sausage

1 Green pepper, chopped

8 Cloves of garlic, minced

¼ Cup fresh basil, chopped

¼ Cup fresh oregano, chopped

2 Tablespoons fresh rosemary, chopped

2 Teaspoons salt

Fresh ground black pepper

Pinch sugar

¼ Cup olive oil

½ Cup red wine, such as Shiraz.

Procedure for meat sauce

Step 1: Add olive oil to a medium sauce pot over a medium high heat. Allow a few minutes for the oil to come up to temp. Add the mushrooms and the Italian sausage. Brown the sausage.

Step 2: Add the green peppers and onions. Sauté until they start becoming translucent. Add the garlic and sauté for one minute until golden.

Step 3: Add the tomatoes and red wine. Stir to combine and bring to a simmer.

Step 4: Add the herbs salt and pepper. Simmer on a low heat, stirring occasionally for 15 minutes.

Step 5: Taste the sauce, if it seems a bit green or bitter, add a pinch of sugar.

Step 6: Allow the sauce to rest and cool for 10 minutes before assembling the lasagna in the pan.

Assembling the lasagna

The number of layers you want is completely up to your personal preference. I've made lasagna that was 8 layers deep of alternating meat sauce and cheese. The more layers you have the more of a role the pasta plays in the flavor and texture of the dish. The fewer layers the more the meat sauce and the cheese play a role.

I wrote this recipe to be 3 layers of pasta and a thick bottom layer of meat sauce, a layer of cheese and a thin top layer of meat sauce. If you want a lot of thin layers you will want to make and roll out more pasta.

Procedure

Step 1: Preheat the oven to 350 degrees.

Step 2: Roll out the pasta so that the bottom layer will be at a number 4 thickness. All other layers will be rolled to a number 3 thickness. Each run of sheets will end up roughly 4 ½ inches wide, so it will take side by side sheets to properly cover the width of the lasagna pan.

Step 3: Ladle a small amount of the meat sauce into the bottom of the lasagna pan along with two tablespoons of olive oil and spread the mixture out. This will help keep the bottom layer from sticking to the pan.

Step 4: On a floured cutting board place the two sheets of number 4 pasta so they are overlapping by a quarter inch. Press or pinch them together with your fingertips to join them. Once they are joined lay them gently into the bottom of the lasagna pan. This is the only layer where you need to pinch the seam.

Step 5: Ladle two-thirds of the meat sauce over the bottom layer of pasta. Spread into an even layer.

Step 6: Lay down two side by side sheets of pasta at a number 3 thickness above the meat layer.

Step 7: Lay out the sliced mozzarella like overlapping shingles. This will ensure that every piece you cut will come out with that telltale stringy cheese.

Step 8: Carefully spoon the ricotta cheese mixture over the sliced mozzarella. Spread it evenly.

Step 9: Cover this layer with another layer of side by side sheets of pasta.

Step 10: Ladle the remaining meat sauce on top and cover with the remaining half pound of grated mozzarella cheese.

Step 11: Place the lasagna pan in a 350 degree oven for 30-45 minutes or until the cheese on top melts and begins to turn golden brown.

Not serving this with garlic bread would be a capital offense in some states. I would pair it with the same Shiraz or similar red wine that you used in the sauce.

Chapter 4 –Ravioli

Ravioli is another Italian classic comfort food. However for the average home cook who doesn't have a lot of experience working with fresh pasta it can be a challenging as well as tedious process. The two biggest challenges are forming the pasta and sealing it.

There are a dozen different gadgets on the market that claim to make shaping ravioli easy. Most of them tend to cause a lot of waste or they squeeze filling onto the seams, making it very hard to get a good seal. Without a proper seal the filling will eventually pour out of the pasta and into the cooking water. I'm sure if you throw enough money at enough of these gadgets you will eventually find one you can live with. Honestly, even the best ones I've seen are only a few minutes faster than doing it the tried and true way by hand.

When rolling out the sheets, thin pasta is easier to work with than thick pasta. At the same time, pasta that is rolled too thin can rip during cooking. Personally I prefer to work with sheets of pasta that have been rolled out on a thickness setting of three.

Ravioli need not be over stuffed. A tablespoon of filling is about the perfect portion for the average diner. Sealing individual ravioli can be tedious. The fresher the pasta sheets are the easier they are to seal and the stronger the seal will be. Some recipes advocate using an egg wash to help bind the two sheets, however this is messy and if you accidentally use too much in just one small spot you open up chances of a leak during cooking.

In my experience I have found that gently, yet firmly pressing the seam with the tines of a fork will give you a good enough seal to handle the three to four minute cook time.

When it comes to fillings, your options are limited only by your imagination. However the two classics that bring the most comfort food magic are Ricotta and Herb, and Spicy Italian Sausage. I've included recipes for both.

Ricotta and Herb Ravioli

Ingredients for filling

1 Cup of ricotta cheese

½ Cup of mozzarella cheese

½ Cup of parmesan cheese

1 Egg yolk

2 Cloves of garlic, minced

¼ Cup of fresh parsley, chopped

1 Tablespoon fresh basil, chopped

1 Tablespoon fresh oregano, chopped

½ Teaspoon sea salt

Fresh cracked black pepper

Procedure for Ricotta and Herb filling

Simply combine all ingredients one hour before you plan to stuff the pasta. This lead time will allow the flavors of the herbs to infuse into the cheese stuffing.

Stuffing the Ravioli

Obviously fresh pasta is a key ingredient for making ravioli at home. Simply use the same procedures from the chapter on making fresh pasta. Roll out into long sheets 4 inches wide at a number 3 thickness setting.

It is easier to work with a pliable freshly rolled strip of pasta. So if you are preparing the ravioli alone, I recommend working with one strip at a time. If you have a partner it is best to split up the tasks so that one person is rolling and stuffing while the other is cutting and sealing.

Equipment

Pizza cutter

Fork

Tablespoon

Large pot of boiling water

Toothpick

Ingredients

Ricotta and Herb filling from above

1 Pound of fresh pasta, cut 4 inches wide and rolled out at a number 3 thickness

Procedure

Step 1: Roll out a single sheet. Use a toothpick to mark where the two inch mid line of the sheet is. Eventually you will fold the top half over the bottom so the simple marking will make it easier for you to find the middle when you make the long fold.

Step 2: In the middle of the bottom half, portion out one mounded tablespoon of filling. Make sure to leave at least 1½ inches of space between each mound of filling.

Step 3: Fold the other side of the pasta strip over the filling. Use your fingers to work out any obvious air bubbles.

Step 4: Use your fingers to lightly pinch down the seam.

Step 5: Cut the individual ravioli free from each other using a pizza cutter.

Step 6: Pinch a fork down along the edges of each ravioli sealing all three seams. Use the fork on the edge without a seam that was rolled over just to give all four sizes the same visual appeal.

Step 7: Giving the seams 10 minutes to bind together before cooking in the boiling water will help them stay together.

Freezing - If you have a large batch you can freeze them in the freezer, uncooked, on a baking sheet and then vacuum seal them for cooking at a later date. They will keep frozen for up to a month. *The faster you freeze them the more of the filling's flavor will come through later. I always turn the freezer up to the highest setting for 2 hours so the blower will speed the freezing process.*

Step 8: Prepare the sauce you want to dress them in. I prefer a classic marinara for the spicy pork and an Alfredo for the cheese and herb filling. Ultimately the sauce should match the filling of your choice.

Step 9: Bring a gallon of water to low boil. Place the ravioli in the water in small batches. After 4-5 minutes they will float. This means they are done.

Step 10: Remove directly from the water and plate with the sauce of your choice. If you are serving a large number of people you should probably use multiple pots of boiling water. Another handy trick is to warm oven safe plates in a 200 degree oven in advance. This ensures that each diner gets a thoroughly warm plate of ravioli.

While the sauce and the filling you choose to dress the ravioli will determine the kind of wine you pair it with, it's always good to top with a little shaved parmesan and chopped parsley.

Spicy Pork Ravioli

While you can easily go to the grocery store and buy a package of ground Italian Sausage without casing, I personally prefer to make my own from scratch. Store made Italian sausage tends to use a heavy hand when seasoning with fennel seed. Since the sausage is ground, packaged and sits, sometimes for days the other flavors become muted and the taste of the fennel seed looms large like an electric guitar solo in a child's lullaby.

Buying plain ground pork and adding the seasoning myself, not only allows me to control the ingredients, it also allows each ingredient to pop in the final product.

Ingredients for Spicy Pork filling

½ Pound of ground pork

4 Cloves of garlic, minced

1 Teaspoon red pepper flakes

½ Medium red onion, minced

1 Tablespoon fresh rosemary, chopped

1 Tablespoon fresh basil, chopped

1 Tablespoon fresh oregano, chopped

½ Teaspoon fennel seed

1 Egg yolk

½ Cup of parmesan cheese

Salt

An aggressive amount of fresh cracked black pepper

Procedure for Spicy Pork filling

Step 1: Brown the ground pork in a medium sauce pan over medium heat. Cook the meat for two minutes then add the herbs, salt, black pepper, red pepper flakes, garlic and onions. Continue stirring until the pork is thoroughly browned.

Step 2: Remove to a medium size work bowl and cool for 10 minutes.

Step 3: Add the egg yolk and parmesan cheese. Toss thoroughly to combine and allow five minutes for the residual heat to integrate the parmesan cheese.

Stuffing Spicy Pork Ravioli

This is the same procedure as it is for stuffing the Ricotta and Herb ravioli.

Obviously fresh pasta is a key ingredient for making ravioli at home. Simply use the same procedures from the chapter on making fresh pasta. Roll out into long sheets 4 inches wide at a number 3 thickness setting.

It is easier to work with a pliable freshly rolled strip of pasta. So if you are preparing the ravioli alone, I recommend working with one strip at a time. If you have a partner it is best to split up the tasks so that one person is rolling and stuffing while the other is cutting and sealing.

Equipment

Pizza cutter

Fork

Tablespoon

Large pot of boiling water

Toothpick

Ingredients

Spicy Pork Ravioli filling

1 Pound of fresh pasta cut 4 inches wide and rolled out at a number 3 thickness

Procedure

Step 1: Roll out a single sheet. Use a toothpick to mark where the two inch mid line of the sheet is. Eventually you will fold the top half over the bottom so the simple marking will make it easier for you to find the middle when you make the long fold.

Step 2: In the middle of the bottom half, portion out one mounded tablespoon of filling. Make sure to leave at least 1½ inches of space between each mound of filling.

Step 3: Fold the other side of the pasta strip over the filling. Use your fingers to work out any obvious air bubbles.

Step 4: Use your fingers to lightly pinch down the seam.

Step 5: Cut the individual ravioli free from each other using a pizza cutter.

Step 6: Pinch a fork down along the edges of each ravioli sealing all three seams. Use the fork on the edge without a seam that was rolled over just to give all four sizes the same visual appeal.

Step 7: Giving the seams 10 minutes to bind together before cooking in the boiling water will help them stay together.

Freezing - If you have a large batch you can freeze them in the freezer, uncooked, on a baking sheet and then vacuum seal them for cooking at a later date. They will keep frozen for up to a month. *The faster you freeze them the more of the filling's flavor will come through later. I always turn the freezer up to the highest setting for 2 hours so the blower will speed the freezing process.*

Step 8: Prepare the sauce you want to dress them in. I prefer a classic marinara for the spicy pork and an Alfredo for the cheese and herb filling. Ultimately the sauce should match the filling of your choice.

Step 9: Bring a gallon of water to low boil. Place the ravioli in the water in small batches. After 4-5 minutes they will float. This means they are done.

Step 10: Remove directly from the water and plate with the sauce of your choice. If you are serving a large number of people you should probably use multiple pots of boiling water. Another handy trick is to warm oven safe plates in a 200 degree oven in advance. This ensures that each diner gets a thoroughly warm plate of ravioli.

While the sauce and the filling you choose to dress the ravioli will determine the kind of wine you pair it with, it's always good to top with a little shaved parmesan and chopped parsley.

Chapter 5 –Spaghetti Bolognese

Spaghetti can be made from fresh pasta by running the sheet of pasta through the cutter setting for spaghetti. Just roll the sheet out to a number 4 thickness and then slowly feed the sheet through the pasta cutter attachment for spaghetti. You could use a number 3 thickness for this as well and you would get vermicelli.

I've found that a number 3 and thinner have a nasty habit of tearing at the worst possible times in the cutting process. Be mindful to go extra slow when cutting pasta this thin.

Drying spaghetti can be challenging. Once the noodles are rolled out try to drape them over a pasta drying rack or lay them out on a paper towel. In all honesty this can be a tedious process and I wouldn't judge you if you just wanted to use dried spaghetti noodles and save the fresh pasta for the larger noodles like ravioli and lasagna.

However if you want to try making spaghetti from fresh pasta and pair it with the sauce that suits it best, then the slow cooked velvet smooth meat sauce known as Bolognese is the way to go. Fresh cut spaghetti should be boiled for no longer than 2 minutes before being incorporated into the sauce. Allowing the pasta to finish in the sauce will saturate the noodles, maximize flavor and highlight the texture of each component.

Bolognese Sauce

You can walk down the aisle of the grocery store and find a jar of spaghetti sauce with meat. You can even find jars of stuff called "Meat Sauce." When you get one home and pour it over a mound of spaghetti the experience can be a bit disappointing. It's not uncommon for people to take that jar of meat sauce and glam it up with extra meat or chopped vegetables. Still at the end of the day using a jar of meat sauce for your spaghetti dinner is like giving your Mom a firm handshake on Mother's Day.

The iconic meat sauce for Spaghetti is the rich velvet smooth magic that is Bolognese. Bolognese is not a tomato sauce with wads of meat curiously suspended in it. Bolognese is a meat sauce with some tomatoes to help brighten the flavor. I'm not going to lie to you. This sauce is another one of those labors of love. To be done right Bolognese is slow cooked to bring out the deep stewed flavors of the meat and give it a smooth texture.

When it comes to choosing the meat, both ground pork and veal have a traditional place in the sauce. I personally favor 80/20 ground chuck and ground pork. You will want to allow at least three hours of prep and cook time before you plan to serve. While you could get away with using a sauce pan and a crockpot on its warmest setting, it is better to use a Dutch oven with an enamel coating.

Equipment

Enamel coated Dutch oven, for preparing the Bolognese

Large sauce pot, for cooking the spaghetti

Colander

Ingredients

1 Large yellow onion, chopped

1 Medium carrot, chopped fine

1 Spear of celery, chopped

6 Cloves of garlic, minced

2 Tablespoons fresh oregano, chopped

4 Tablespoons olive oil

½ Pound ground beef or chuck

½ Pound ground pork

1 Cup of cream or half & half

1 Cup of medium red wine, Shiraz

28 ounces of diced tomato

Salt and fresh cracked black pepper

Parmesan cheese

Fresh parsley, chopped

Procedure

Step 1: Heat the olive oil a Dutch oven over medium heat. When the oil shimmers add the onions, carrots and celery. Sweat for 5 minutes.

Step 2: Add the minced garlic and sweat for approximately two minutes or until the garlic starts to take on a golden brown color.

Step 3: Add a half cup of the diced tomatoes and do not stir them at first. Allow them to sear a little bit onto the bottom of the pot, this will give the tomato added depth of flavor and body in the final sauce.

Step 4: Add the ground meat in small batches, crumbling it into the pot. Toss the meat as it browns.

Step 5: Reduce the heat to the lowest possible setting and add the half & half along with the oregano. Simmer for 10 minutes.

Step 6: Add half of the tomatoes and the red wine. Simmer for 10 minutes allowing the wine to incorporate its flavor into the meat while also unlocking the alcohol soluble flavor compounds in the tomatoes.

Step 7: Add the remaining tomatoes and stir to incorporate.

Step 8: Keep the heat on low. You want to simmer this sauce at a temperature slightly hotter than a warm smile. This slow stewing will give make the sauce smooth like velvet while also building hearty flavors.

Step 9: Bring a gallon of water to a boil in a large sauce pot. Once it is boiling add the spaghetti. I find a quarter pound of spaghetti per diner to be about the right amount.

Step 10: Boil the spaghetti until it is 80% soft. Then strain the water from the pasta using a colander. Return the pasta to the pot on low heat. Ladle the sauce over the top of the spaghetti until you are happy with the sauce to pasta ratio. Allow the spaghetti to finish cooking in the sauce.

Step 11: Plate the spaghetti, ladle any additional sauce over the top. Garnish with shaved parmesan cheese and chopped parsley.

When it comes to side dishes I recommend something with earthy flavors. Sautéed mushrooms or broiled asparagus are perfect compliments to the bold meaty flavors of the Bolognese. For a wine pairing, while I recommend using Shiraz in the sauce to wake up the flavors, you could find any red that matches the beef flavor profile of the Bolognese.

Chapter 6 –Pasta Aglio e Olio (a new take on a classic recipe)

Directly translated Pasta Aglio e Olio means pasta with garlic and oil. The oil in question is of course extra-virgin olive oil and the pasta usually is a dry pasta strand variety such as vermicelli or spaghetti. In its simplest form Pasta Aglio e Olio is just cooked spaghetti tossed with some high quality olive oil and fresh garlic, garnished with salt, black pepper and fresh chopped parsley.

Since Italy is a land of regional cuisine it stands to reason that there are a lot of variations available to the intrepid home chef. This interpretation is my Americanized take on a dish from the Amalfi Coast, which is a cuisine that is heavy with fresh or cured anchovies. In all honesty trying to get your hands on quality, fresh or cured anchovies in the United States can be a high priced labor of love. An interesting twist that I have grown fond of is to use lightly smoked white fish with some pickled pepperoncini peppers for brightness and life.

The olive oil is a critical ingredient in this dish and it's worth spending a little extra to get the good stuff. Because the olive oil is a major part of the flavor and texture it's also a good idea to serve the dish in a warmed serving bowl. In a pinch you can use a Pyrex lasagna pan heated ahead of time in a warm oven.

The proportion between the oil and the amount of pasta is a critical relationship for the dish to come out properly balanced. This recipe assumes a quarter pound of spaghetti per diner for four diners. If you have more or less diners be sure to adjust all the ingredients accordingly.

Adding the garlic in two different phases accents its sautéed flavors as well as the heat and bite of fresh garlic.

Equipment

A large sauce pan

A large sauce pot

Tongs

Oven safe serving dish or Pyrex baking pan

Ingredients

½ Cup of extra-virgin olive oil

8 Cloves of garlic, minced

2 Cloves of garlic, sliced thin

½ Teaspoon red pepper flake

4 Pickled Pepperoncini peppers, chopped

2 Tablespoons of capers

1 Shallot, minced

¼ Cup of cherry tomatoes, halved and seeded

¼ Cup of Kalamata olives

2 Tablespoons of lemon juice

Sea Salt and fresh cracked black pepper

1 Medium fillet of smoked white fish

Procedure

Step 1: White Fish can be bony, so it is best before starting to hand pick the meat from the bone the reserve it in a small dish in the refrigerator.

Step 2: Place an oven safe serving bowl or Pyrex baking pan in an oven preheated to 200 degrees.

Step 3: Bring one gallon of water to a boil in a large sauce pot over medium-high heat. When it comes to a boil add the spaghetti.

Step 4: Pour the olive oil into a large sauce pan over medium heat. Add the shallots, minced garlic, and tomatoes. Toss continuously until the garlic begins to take a little color. Approximately 5 minutes.

Step 5: Add the Kalamata olives, capers, red pepper flakes and pepperoncini peppers. Toss to combine for another 2 minutes to heat the olives and peppers through.

Step 6: Add the white fish meat and reduce the heat to low.

Step 7: When the pasta is cooked soft, drain through a colander. Do not rinse. Move pasta directly to the pan and toss it in the oil.

Step 8: Add the sliced garlic, salt and pepper to taste.

Step 9: Pull the serving bowl from the oven. Pour the pasta into the bowl and garnish with a squirt of lemon juice, shaved parmesan and fresh chopped parsley.

This dish is best paired with a bright acidic white wine such as Pinot Grigio or Riesling. Soft white bread is better than toasted garlic bread or crostini as you can use the soft bread to pinch the flavorful oil left on the plate at the end of the meal.

Chapter 7 –Linguine with Clam Sauce

Linguine is the middle child of strand noodles. Linguine sits between wide flat fettuccine and narrow round spaghetti. While you can buy linguine in dry strands, it really does incorporate into sauces better when you make it fresh. Most pasta cutter attachments have a setting for linguine just one notch narrower than the fettuccine setting. Or you can simply cut fettuccine and then halve each noodle the long way with a sharp knife. Linguine should be roughly 1/8 to 1/4 of an inch wide.

Clam Sauce

While the stereotypical image of Italy is a land rife with pasta and tomatoes, it should not be ignored that it is a country with a lot of coast line and a passionate love affair with seafood. Grandma used to tell me stories of days back in the old country when Papa would get in a long boat and head out on the water to catch what they were going to eat that day. Often this was a jab at how poor a fisherman he was, but it always gave her an excuse to get him out of her hair while she shopped the docks for fresh shellfish.

We've all heard of the dish linguini with clam sauce, yet a lot of Italian restaurant franchises don't even have it on their menu. The restaurants that usually do have it are either near a coast or they are a mom and pop establishment that isn't turning over too many covers in the course of a night.

The main problem is the high cost of quality clam meat. In this case were talking about little neck clams. Sure you can buy a can of clam meat and use it for the sauce but it's a little bit like buying a can of dog food to add to your meatloaf. Another alternative is to use larger chowder clams. In regards to meat, this is still a step down in quality. However, the clam juice in a large chowder clam is exactly the same as in the small tender little neck clam.

If you live in an area where little neck clams are expensive, I advocate using a mixture of little neck clams and chowder clams. Once the chowder clams release their juice into the sauce simply remove them. Since chowder clams are so cheap there's little guilt from throwing them away. If you are into gardening, they will be a nice addition to the compost pile when crushed.

Typically this dish is thought of with linguine. However the frilly bell shaped campanelle or the twirls of rotini can be a great pasta pairing. I personally think their contours and textures do a better job of holding onto the sauce than linguine.

Equipment

A medium stock pot

A large sauce pot

Steamer basket

2 Medium sized work bowls

Slotted spoon

Cheese cloth

Fine mesh strainer with handle

Ingredients

½ pound of little neck clams per diner

½ pound of chowder clams per diner

1 Cup of Pinot Grigio or similar white wine

½ Teaspoon red pepper flake

1 Teaspoon Old Bay seasoning

4 Cloves of garlic, minced

1 Shallot, chopped fine

½ Cup of Cherry tomatoes, halved and seeded

½ Cup fresh parsley, chopped

¼ Pound of linguine (or alternate pasta) per diner.

Procedure

Step 1: Bring a gallon of water to a boil in a large sauce pot.

Step 2: Place a medium stock pot over medium-high heat. You want to make sure the pot can hold all of the clams at one time. Add the chowder clams, wine, red pepper flake and Old Bay seasoning. Insert the steamer basket above the chowder clams and place the little neck clams in it.

Step 3: Leave the lid off so you can watch the pot carefully. Every 30 seconds or so give the pot a little shake. After 3-5 minutes the little neck clams will begin to open and release their juice. Remove them immediately with a slotted spoon. Reserve them in a medium sized work bowl.

Step 4: Once all the little neck clams have opened remove the steamer basket and place the lid on the pot. After 3 minutes lift the lid and check to see if the chowder clams have opened. Simmer for

3-5 minutes or until all chowder clams have opened. Once they have opened, remove them and discard or reserve in the refrigerator to make a small batch of chowder the next day.

Step 5: Line a fine mesh strainer with cheese cloth. Pour the clam liquor through the cheese cloth, holding the strainer over a medium sized work bowl. The cheese cloth should catch any trace amount of grit released by the clams.

Step 6: In the large sauce pan heat the olive oil over medium low heat. When it shimmers add the garlic, shallots and tomatoes. Heat for 5 minutes or until the garlic turns golden brown.

Step 7: Place the pasta in the boiling water and cook until they are al dente.

Step 8: Add the little neck clams to the large sauce pan and turn the heat up to medium-high. Allow the little neck clams to come up to heat for 2 minutes.

Step 9: Add the clam liquor.

Step 10: Strain the pasta and add it directly to the large sauce pan. Reduce the heat to low and toss to combine.

Step 11: Garnish with pasta and serve immediately.

The remaining Pinot Grigio when chilled is a perfect pairing for this dish.

Chapter 8 –Linguine Carbonara

Carbonara sauce is almost more suited to breakfast than it is lunch or supper. The presence of eggs, cheese and bacon makes it a natural player in the morning. I have honestly made this dish for breakfast in the morning before heading out to fortify me on a big project day.

This is not the kind of dish that you wait on. In order to keep it from congealing it needs to go from pot to serving bowl to plate as fast as humanly possible. In fact, for your serving bowl I recommend something you can warm in the oven, such as a Pyrex lasagna pan.

It's also important to note that the eggs are the base of the sauce and the egg sauce should be poured over the piping hot pasta not the other way around. This recipe is designed to serve four people. The proportion of egg to pasta is important. The intended portion calls for a quarter pound of Linguine per diner. If you have more or less than four diners, you must adjust all the ingredients accordingly or the sauce will not be balanced.

If you are concerned about using raw egg and the potential that you might not get it cooked through the first time you try it, simply use pasteurized eggs.

Equipment

Medium work bowl

Large sauce pot

Medium frying pan

Oven safe serving bowl

Tongs

Colander

Ingredients

2 Tablespoons of extra virgin olive oil

1 pound of bacon, cut into bite sized pieces

½ Cup of white wine, Pinot Grigio

4 large eggs

4 Cloves of garlic minced

½ Red onion, minced

2 Tablespoons fresh parsley, chopped

1 Cup of grated Romano or Parmesan cheese

Salt

Teaspoon of fresh cracked black pepper

1 Pound of Linguine

Procedure

Step 1: Place your oven safe serving bowl or lasagna pan in an oven preheated to 200 degrees.

Step 2: Cut up the bacon into bite sized pieces and begin frying. You want to bring them to the point where they are medium crisp after most of the fat has rendered out of them. Once they are done frying remove them to a paper towel and tent the paper towel with tinfoil to help hold in some of the heat.

Step 3: While the bacon is frying bring a gallon of water to rolling boil. Once boiling, add the Linguine.

Step 4: Once the bacon is done frying, pour off any excess grease. Reduce the heat to medium low and add the red onions and white wine to the pan. Simmer for 3 minutes to mellow the alcohol flavor.

Step 5: Add the bacon back into the pan and allow it to take up some of the sweet notes of the wine. Simmer for 5 minutes. The wine should almost completely reduce and infuse into the onions and bacon.

Step 6: Add the eggs to a large work bowl and whisk aggressively to make them as smooth as possible.

Step 7: Add the cheese, garlic, salt, pepper, chopped parsley and olive oil to the egg. Whisk to combine.

Step 8: When the pasta is cooked al dente, remove the warmed serving bowl from the oven. Strain the pasta through a colander and add it immediately to the warmed serving bowl.

Step 9: Pour the egg mixture over the top of the pasta and toss quickly to combine. The heat of the pasta will gently cook the egg as you combine it.

Step 10: Add the wine infused onions and bacon. Toss one last time to combine. Serve immediately.

This dish begs for soft scarpetta bread to be served alongside it so you can mop up the sauce with the soft bread. The same Pinot

Grigio that you used to infuse the onions and bacon will also pair well with the Carbonara so long as it is properly chilled.

Chapter 9 –Fettuccine Alfredo

Fettuccine Alfredo made from dried pasta and a jarred sauce is something you can throw together and it will be edible. I would honestly say that it is better than some of my early botched attempts at making this dish with fresh pasta and scratch made sauce. If you're a rookie at making a cream sauce you are almost sure to screw this up the first time. However once you get it right and develop a feel for it, this dish has the same comfort food magic as fresh baked bread or buttery mashed potatoes.

It is worth stumbling the first few times in order to enjoy this scratch made dish for a lifetime.

While the sauce is the hardest part of the dish, we shouldn't overlook the fettuccine. One of the important things about this dish is the pastas ability to absorb the sauce and develop a relationship in flavor and texture. Dried fettuccine is not very absorbent and sort of languishes in the sauce, often sticking to itself more than the sauce.

Fettuccine made from fresh pasta, then cooked partially in water and allowed to finish in the sauce is superior in flavor as well as texture. Simply roll out the pasta to a 1/8th inch thickness on the number 5 setting of your pasta roller machine. Then lightly flour, loosely role and cut into half inch width. Or pass it through the fettuccine size of the pasta cutter attachment.

Alfredo sauce is like dancing the Waltz. On paper you're making a bunch of simple movements that keep you and your partner in synch. When both partners are intuitively in step with each other every motion is velvet smooth. If they are out of step, they eventually trip and join the clump of other bad dancers that hang out at the edges of the dance floor.

It's worth noting that pasteurized cream from the organic foods section of the grocery store has a better flavor than ultra-pasteurized cream. This recipe assumes that there will be four diners, each with a quarter pound portion of pasta.

Equipment

Large sauce pot

Large sauce pan

Colander

Silicone spatula

Ingredients

1 ½ Cups of pasteurized heavy cream

4 Tablespoons of butter

2 Cloves of minced garlic

1 Cup of parmesan cheese, freshly grated

1 Tablespoon of lemon juice

Salt

Fresh cracked black pepper

1 Pound of Fettuccine (for 4 diners)

Procedure

Step 1: After making the fresh fettuccine. Bring one gallon of salted water to a full boil in a large sauce pot.

Step 2: Melt the butter and add the minced garlic in a large sauce pan over low heat.

Step 3: When the butter is melted add one cup of the pasteurized cream and bring it to a low simmer.

Step 4: Add the fresh pasta to the boiling water and cook until al dente, approximately 5 minutes. You don't want to cook the pasta all the way. When it is 75% cooked, drain the pasta in a colander and add it directly to the large sauce pan. Reduce the heat to low.

Step 5: Add the fresh cracked black pepper along with the lemon juice and the last half cup of cream. Stir to combine.

Step 6: Sprinkle a little of the parmesan cheese into the pan, fold with a silicone spatula. Continue to sprinkle and fold again. Repeat until all the parmesan is incorporated.

Step 7: Cook on low heat for 2 minutes before plating.

This pasta dish can stand alone with a big piece of garlic bread. It can also be a large meal when paired with a roasted chicken breast and some steamed broccoli. A chilled glass of chardonnay pairs perfectly.

Chapter 10 –Baked Ziti

Baked Ziti is probably the most popular dish from a family of dishes called Al Forno. Al Forno is a technique used for partially cooking pasta in water then saucing it and baking it in the oven to finish. Baked Ziti when it's done right is a hearty meal that is easy to serve up family style. When done wrong it's a strange glop of flabby over cooked pasta, with sauce sliding off every forkful.

Making ziti from scratch is relatively easy. Simply roll out a sheet of pasta at a number 4 or 5 setting. Roll it the short way along a plastic straw or smooth chopstick that has been greased with olive oil. When the seam meets the rest of the sheet, cut it with a dough scraper. Roll it back and forth gently 3 times to pinch the seam. Then carefully slide the chop stick out of the pasta tube. Then cut the tubes into 1-1/2 inch lengths.

The most important thing here is the balance in cooking time. Ziti is rather easy to make from fresh pasta but because it starts out soft already the window for perfect doneness in the oven is narrower. For this reason I suggest making the following dish with dried pasta a couple of times to get a feel for all of the other procedures before making ziti from fresh pasta. While the fresh pasta version is much better at integrating with the sauce the dry pasta is still an acceptable compromise.

The following recipe is for dried pasta. If you make the dish with fresh rolled pasta you will completely skip the boiling procedure of the recipe. For fresh ziti simple make all noodles, place them in the refrigerator while you prepare the marinara sauce and then add them dry to the sauce when you prepare to put it in the oven.

For the sauce simply follow the classic marinara recipe we discussed earlier.

There are a lot of different recipes out there talking about adding meatballs, sausages and a myriad of vegetables to the sauce. The problem is they will all increase the baking time, which of course increases the chance that you will over cook the pasta into a pile of flabby noodle. Therefore, if you are going to add extra ingredients to the basic recipe you should completely cook them through in advance before adding them into the sauce. Here is the recipe for assembling the baked ziti:

Equipment

13 X 9 baking dish

Large sauce pot of boiling water

Colander

Tongs

Ingredients

A batch of classic marinara sauce (see chapter 2)

One pound of ziti (dried or fresh)

2 Teaspoons of salt

12 Ounces of mozzarella cheese, shredded

¾ Cup of Romano cheese, grated

3 Tablespoons of fresh parsley, chopped

Procedure

Step 1: Preheat the oven to 400 degrees, while preparing the classic marinara sauce.

Step 2: Bring a pot of water to a boil with a gallon of water and two teaspoons of salt over medium-high heat.

Step 3: Add the dried pasta to the water. Cook until it is still toothsome, approximately 5 minutes. You do not want to cook it to completion. You should be able to take a simple tubular noodle, squeeze down on it lightly and it should just flatten without cracking the tube.

Step 4: Drain the pasta through a colander and return it to the pot with the heat off. Immediately add the marinara sauce. Fold the noodles and sauce together gently.

Step 5: Lightly oil the 13 x 9 baking pan.

Step 6: Add a third of the pasta and sauce mixture to the pan and spread evenly.

Step 7: Sprinkle with one third of the mozzarella and one third of the Romano cheese.

Step 8: Repeat steps 6 and 7 until all the pasta, sauce and cheese has been added to the baking pan in layers.

Step 9: Place the baking pan in the 400 degree oven for 15 minutes or until the cheese is golden brown.

This dish is made to be served with scarpetta or soft, fresh baked bread. It pairs well with a medium red wine like Shiraz or Pinot Noir.

Conclusion

Learning how to make pasta and classic Italian sauces can be a challenge at first. So much of it is about honoring and understanding the ingredients and the relationship the sauce has to the pasta. At the same time it is a journey that rewards you along the way.

With these recipes you can begin to understand these tender relationships and how you want to play with pairings between classical combinations as well decorative pastas. Armed with a little authentic experience your kitchen table will only be limited by your imagination.

Part II - Growing and Cooking Italian Vegetables

Gardening Tips and Recipes from a Lifetime of Italian Cooking

Introduction

When I was a child my mother worked a lot of double shifts. While she was slaving away in a hot factory I was looked after by the elderly Italian woman who lived next door. She and her husband were immigrants who came to America after World War Two. They spent most of their adult lives running an Italian restaurant. They retired to the house next door just a few weeks before I was born.

Since my own Grandparents had passed away years earlier, I came to call them Grandma and Papa. While the blood on both sides of my family is German, my childhood in Grandma's kitchen gave me an Italian soul.

Each morning Grandma would take me to the garden. I would follow along at her side as she tended to an immense assortment of herbs, tomatoes and peppers. As she weaved from row to row it was always my job to hold the picking basket. She always started in the tomatoes, before picking her way through ripe peppers and finishing up in the verdant maze of fresh herbs.

As she handed each tomato and pepper over to me I would hold it for a moment under my nose and smell the pungent green freshness before putting it into the basket. I have wonderful memories of staring down at the basket full of fresh picked vegetables knowing that they would become my lunch and supper.

She sang classic Italian songs as she washed the vegetables. I never understood the lyrics but they were a lullaby soothing me down for my morning nap. As soon as she was done washing everything she would scoop me up and lay me down in my day bed.

I would get up from my nap an hour later and lunch was served. Lunch was usually a steaming bowl of fresh pasta enrobed in rich marinara sauce that she would garnished with melting cheese and fresh herbs. I would devour meatballs the size of my head and sop up red sauce with fluffy hunks of scarpetta bread.

Many people talk of their childhood memories with evocative descriptions of chocolate chip cookies, chicken noodle and colorful sugary cereals. For me it was those memories of Italian classics made from scratch.

Unfortunately Grandma and Papa passed away shortly before my 9th birthday. Daily meals of scratch made Italian classics, fresh baked bread and aromatic herbs was ripped from my life. It was replaced by a soul rending menu that mostly consisted of cans of ravioli, frozen pizza and grainy microwave hamburgers.

I have spent years of trial and error in the kitchen, guided by my memories as I learn to recreate her cooking. I found very quickly that the difference between vegetables from the grocery store compared to vegetables fresh picked from the garden is night and day. This meant if I was going to create the magic of her tomato ragu, I was going to have to learn to grow San Marzano tomatoes. If I was ever going to sink my teeth into a thick salty cube of eggplant parmesan, I was going to have to learn to grow Rosa Bianca Eggplant.

One of the things that makes Italian cooking such a favorite at so many restaurant and kitchen tables is that to really do it right you have to use the freshest and best ingredients. You honor those ingredients by preparing them with care. The end result is a dish where everyone at your table can taste the love.

This is a product of putting in the time to learn how to grow and cultivate vegetables and herbs or find them at farmer's markets and grocery stores. Sure, you can get these things from a jarred sauce or a freezer case box of something but it's going to be the cooking equivalent of ending a hot date with handshake instead of a long kiss goodnight.

Even if you are not interested in Italian cooking, these basic vegetables translate into many other recipes and types of cuisine.

The information that follows is from my own experience and research. It's worth noting that I am not some master chef who studied in Naples. I am not hocking my knowledge to become the next celebrity chef with a cooking show and a spiffy catch phrase.

I am essentially just like you. I work a daily grind, I try to raise my daughter right, I work on the side as a freelance writer and I cook almost all of the meals my family eats from scratch.

Chapter 1 – Heirloom versus Hybrid

To the average person heirloom vegetables is a term often thrown around loosely to indicate something of quality. You rarely ever see heirloom vegetables in the grocery store and when you do it's usually a display of tomatoes marked with an astronomical price. If you gave in to the temptation to pick through the display, you probably found a motley assortment of bruised tomatoes that looked like they were two minutes away from turning bad.

If you had that kind of experience at the grocery store I would completely understand why you might be put off the notion that heirloom vegetables actually are something of quality.

Hybrid vegetables, like the ones you can find year round in the grocery store, are manmade creations. Big agricultural companies make the seeds in controlled conditions. They combine two different phenotypes of a vegetable in order to create a seed which will grow a plant with a high yield, durability for mechanical picking and a long shelf life. Flavor is a secondary consideration that often goes ignored or untapped. A lot of the aspects of a vegetable that are related to flavor, such as sugar content, are bad for shelf life.

Since hybrid seeds are effectively mules, they do not breed true. This means if you take that perfectly round, smooth tomato from the grocery store and save its seeds to plant for next year, you will not get the same thing. Roughly 20% of all hybrid seeds even germinate. The one's that do germinate grow slow, twisted and weak. Most that make it to an adult age fail to flower or produce fruit.

Heirloom vegetables are technically open pollinators. An open pollinator is a plant that breeds true. Meaning you can save the seeds from one generation to the next and most of the time you will get exactly the same plant as the parent. The technical distinction for the term Heirloom refers to the fact that the plant has a history which dates back to before 1940. For our purposes going forward I'll use the word heirloom as a short hand to describe all open pollinators.

While hybrid vegetables are made by seed companies and pollinated by interns wearing white lab coats in a sterile facility. Heirloom vegetables are the product of nature. They are pollinated by the magic of wind and bees.

Of course human beings still have a hand in the process. There is a certain organic art to the chaos of how genes carry from one plant to the next. I personally devised a tracking system that I use to select the best seeds from the best plants. So the hand of man is not free from the process. We are still able to choose which traits go forward to the next generation.

Only a small percentage of heirloom vegetables are capable of surviving life in a large apathetic farm field. Most can't handle being picked by a mechanized harvester, packed ten deep in a box and set out for a week in a grocery store display. Long story short, your best bet for finding heirloom vegetables is either at a Farmer's Market during peak season or growing them yourself.

If you choose to grow your own, the good news is, finding a reputable vendor who sells heirloom seeds has never been easier. When I first started acquiring heirloom seeds in the late 90's they were always a clandestine affair. It was always something where a friend of a friend knew a guy who was selling some really primo heirloom zucchini seeds. Then I'd end up at an abandoned barn somewhere meeting a farmer wearing overalls and no tee shirt, looking over his shoulder as if he was waiting for something to happen.

These days you can find a smattering of heirloom seeds in garden supply stores. If you go online there is an enormous variety of seed exchanges and co-op networks selling old classics as well as new cross pollinated varieties of seeds that will breed true.

When it comes to finding seeds, a quick flip through a seed catalog can excite the imagination. My suggestion is to pick one, maybe two vendors at the most to order from to save on shipping. There is sometimes as much as a 100% markup to purchase a single pack of seeds. After that most vendors go by weight, so often times you'll pay the same amount in shipping for five packs of seeds as you would with one.

Chapter 2 – Setting up your seedlings

If you've read my book on growing and cooking herbs then a lot of this chapter will be familiar. While there are many differences between taking care of herbs and taking care of vegetable seedlings a lot of the basic equipment and principles for starting vegetables from seeds are the same as starting herbs from seeds.

I admit that developing a green thumb is to a home gardener what finding your voice is for an aspiring writer. It doesn't always come easy, it might take a little more forethought than you expect and you're going to have to learn from your mistakes along the way.

Most vegetables are easy to start from seed. On a practical level, however, some vegetables are just easier to buy from the nursery. Later when we get to the specific vegetable entries I'll include notes on sourcing seeds versus plants.

This chapter will focus on the basic set up you will need to start vegetables from seeds indoors.

While each type of vegetable might have its own special needs through the course of the season, most will germinate with a little heat, water, light and peat moss.

Seed Starting Kits

A lot of stores these days begin offering seed starter kits (sometimes called heated miniature greenhouses, or heated potting trays) as early as January.

The kit comes with an electric warming mat resting in a protective base tray. Sitting on top of the heat mat is a domed potting tray full of small rehydrated peat moss seed plugs. When the peat moss plugs are properly hydrated and the warming mat is plugged in it supplies a gentle heat to the soil.

The constant heat supply is set around 72 to 75 degrees. The removable domed top of the potting tray keeps moisture from evaporating away. When you set the unit under grow lights or the sunlight from a window with a southern exposure, the seeds will be in optimal conditions for germination.

Most of the time when you buy the kit it is an all in one package that is already filled with dehydrated peat moss seed plugs in it. Every year you can buy new plugs and reuse the rest of the kit. Just speaking from my own experience they generally start to lose a little something in the heating element after six years of heavy use.

Different vegetables may have different start times before the season. So make sure you know how soon to start the seeds before the average last frost date for your region. If you don't know the average last frost date for your area, you can usually find it by contacting or searching your state's agricultural extension office.

While some vegetables, like cabbage and peas can survive temperatures down to twenty degrees, most vegetables seedlings will not tolerate even a light frost on their delicate leaves.

Location

While it's true that you could stick your potting tray and grow lights in any old basement closet and have modest success. There are a few factors to consider that will improve your chances of having strong healthy plants for your summer garden.

Once seedlings germinate they will crave light. Even a strong grow light placed too high overhead will encourage a plant to grow its stem too long, become leggy and fall over. So you will want a location that allows you to adjust the height of your grow lights so that the bulbs are always two to four inches above the highest leaves of the plant.

You also want to have an area available outside of the heated potting tray. While some herbs crave bottom heat on their roots and will thrive, others will begin to get leggy if heat is kept in the soil plug for more than a day or two after germination.

For non-heat loving herbs you will want to remove them from the potting tray within 24 hours of germinating and pot them up into whatever seedling pot you have chosen for them to grow in until it is time for them to be transplanted into the garden.

I have a 24 inch by 48 inch wire bakers rack with adjustable shelves that I use every spring for potting up seedlings. The wire shelves allow me to hook things on, adjust chains or store all the little odds and ends I need without cluttering up the main potting shelf.

Choosing, installing and using grow lights

These days there are a lot of options you can choose from when it comes to grow lights. There is enough science behind it to give you a nose bleed.

Here is a quick summary of your available options and what you need to know.

Plasma: This is a new form of grow light technology. It claims to have the best efficiency and best spectrum of light. From my initial research into the cost, energy usage and the amount of area a single average light can cover, this appears to be more of a commercial grow light.

LED: When LED grow lights first appeared in the marketplace a lot of technical promises were made that ultimately under delivered. While the technology, spectrum range and efficiency has improved rapidly in recent years LED lights can still be a pretty large upfront investment for something as simple as starting seedlings indoors.

High Intensity Discharge: This is probably the most common type of grow light. It is efficient and comes in two different options, Metal Halide and High Pressure Sodium. For starting seedlings and over wintering herbs indoors you will want the Metal Halide Bulbs, which cast towards the blue end of the spectrum. High Pressure Sodium Lights tend to cast in the yellow end of the spectrum meant to mimic waning light of the fall season, which triggers flowering and fruiting plants to bloom. High pressure sodium lights tend to be used by people who grow vegetables indoors all year long.

Fluorescent: This is by far the cheapest and easiest of your grow light options. You will want to buy Full spectrum daylight bulbs, which cost around $10 each and from my experience they have an average lifespan of six years. Any standard 48 inch shop light fixture will hold the bulbs and costs between $15 and $20.The bulbs and the fixtures commonly go on sale in a lot of hardware stores in early February.

Personally I have been using a four fixture Fluorescent grow light system that I cobbled together years ago for $60. In the last seven years I have lost one fixture and one bulb, as a result of a spill while watering.

Window Box: In the spring of 2005 I planted more aggressively than my grow light space allowed. As a result I was forced to start and grow forty plants in a window with a great southern exposure. I can tell you from personal experience that it is possible to start and grow strong plants for a few weeks in a sunny window. In fact only two plants died in the window box before planting day.

It is obviously the cheapest option available to you if you have a window with a good southern exposure. Ironically it is also the most labor intensive. Since young seedlings crave light, they will bend and reach for the strongest light source. If you don't rotate each seedling at least once per day it will cause them to reach too far and become leggy. A leggy plant can easily die if allowed to lean for too long. Even if it survives, the weak stem can struggle against strong summer winds in the garden.

Placing a dozen or so plants on small trays or old cookie sheets is a fast option for rotating the plants.

If you do not have a window with a strong southern exposure you can get by with an eastern exposure. Seedlings will be most hungry for light in the morning. A pure western exposure encourages legging.

Preparing and planting your seed plugs

Once you've established where you want to keep your seed tray you will need to rehydrate the seed plugs. The seed plugs start out as little coins of peat moss that you have to soak in water and they will expand for planting.

There are essentially two different types of soil plugs you can choose from, netted or non-netted. I always choose the netted kind, which comes wrapped in a small mesh that expands when the plug is rehydrated. The fine holes expand easily for the roots to escape when the seedling is potted up to a larger planter. The non-netted kind can sometimes flake apart as the roots expand or can get wedged in the tray and break off when you pull them out.

Usually the instructions that come with the kit tell you place the dehydrated peat moss coins into little slots and fill the tray with warm water. The peat moss coins will slowly expand into soil plugs that are held in place by the plastic slots. I've personally found that this can be a problem since sometimes the soil plugs don't absorb all of the water in the tray. It can be a real pain to try to pour away or bail out the excess water.

What I prefer is to use a small pail or ice cream bucket filled with warm water. I put the exact number of dried plugs into the water for the type of vegetable I'm planting at that time. Then I plant using the following procedure.

Step 1: The plugs will take five minutes to rehydrate. While they are expanding in the water, open your seed packet and dole out two to three times the number of seeds onto a sheet of white paper. I always plant at least double the number of seeds in case of germination failure. If all of them germinate I will later cull or remove the weaker plant by snipping it off where the root meets the stem.

Step 2: When the seed plugs are expanded place them in their spot in the potting tray. If you chose the mesh wrapped style of plugs gently use your fingers to fully open the mesh on top. Then use a tooth pick to rough up the top quarter inch of peat moss.

Step 3: Carefully place the seeds into the peat moss and lightly sink them into the plug. The general rule of thumb is to plant the seed three times deeper than the diameter of the seed. Rarely will you exceed a half inch.

Repeat these steps for each type of herb you are planting. Then cover the potting tray with the clear plastic dome and plug in the heat mat.

While the germination time for each type of vegetable can vary. Usually a seed in the starter kit will germinate in the first 7-14 days. I've had Aji Dulce peppers take as long as four weeks and I've had cherry tomatoes germinate in 3 days.

When a seedling first emerges it craves light and since some seeds actually require light to germinate, I will turn on the grow lights or place the kit in a window box immediately after planting. It's a low feeling to come home from work and find that a little pepper sprouted only to fall over and die from a lack of light.

Seedling Pots

There are a lot of different options available when it comes to selecting the pot for your seedlings. In a pinch I've even used a 22 ounce red solo drink cup with a couple of pin holes in the bottom!

The tender roots of young plants can be subject to transplant shock when removed from their seedling pot. A plastic seedling pot is a cheap option but it increases the chances of transplant shock during the plant's first week in the garden. For some vegetables like cabbage and broccoli transplant shock is nearly a nonfactor. For tender root vegetables like squash and cucumbers transplant shock out of a plastic seed pot is a very strong possibility.

The ideal seed pot is one that biodegrades shortly after planting in the garden. There are several options available to you in the form of peat pots. These pots are made from dried and compressed peat moss. When planted in the moist soil of the garden they begin to break up and allow the plant's roots to grow through them within a week or so.

For the do-it-yourselfer there is the option of making your own pots from newspaper. The Newspaper option will indeed save you money but it will also cost you time and hassle. The basic premise is to find an object like a large tomato can or a wine bottle and wrap multiple layers of newspaper around it. Then secure the seams with paper tape or organic white glue.

Paper mache is also an option for shaping and securing a pot made from newspaper and can be a fun way to dragoon your children into helping you. They get to feel like they are a part of the process and take part in watching their little plant grow. You get nimble little fingers that help save you time.

If you choose to make your own seedling pots from newspaper you will want to make sure the newspaper you source is printed with soy based inks and the tape or glue you use is biodegradable. Most non-glossy newsprint these days is made with inexpensive soy based inks but a quick call to the newspaper will confirm it for you.

Having worked with homemade newspaper pots in the past, they are not the ideal for herbs that will spend more than two to three weeks indoors. After successive watering the newspaper tends to break down and weaken. It often splits at the seam or in the middle of the pot.

Since most vegetables need to be started six to ten weeks before planting, you will ultimately have to put a newspaper based pot inside of a plastic container in order to make up for the structural weakness. Or take the paper mache option.

Size

When it comes to selecting the size of seed pot you want to use, bigger is almost always better. As a good rule of thumb, I wouldn't advise going smaller than a 4 inch diameter seed pot for any vegetable. If you've got the space, a six inch diameter pot would be even better! For some plants such as tomatoes, a tall pot is also preferable because potting deeper allows new roots to sprout from the stem.

Soil

While the peat moss of the soil plugs is the ideal medium for germinating plants and giving young tender roots something to grab ahold of, it is still low in nutrients. A sterile potting mix is preferable to using soil from the garden. Garden soil can hide fungus spores and pests that a young seedling lacks the strength to resist.

It is possible to mix garden soil with vermiculite and a little sand and sterilize it in small batches in a 180 degree oven. You don't want to heat it over 180 degrees because it might damage the chemical structure of key soil nutrients. Test the temperature of the soil by inserting a meat probe into the middle of the batch. I can also tell you from experience that you should not expect a smile on their face when your spouse comes home to a house that stinks of burning dirt!

Chapter 3 – Planning for garden and kitchen

In early January, seed catalogs begin flooding mailboxes as a world of opportunities and ideas explodes into a gardener's imagination. It's easy to thumb through pages and pages of lush green photography full of gardening articles and end up with a too-long laundry list of things you want to grow.

I have to admit that more than once I have gotten myself in over my head by trying to grow too many plants in a greenhouse too small for all my great ideas. I start out every year making a garden plan. I draw out my garden in scale on graph paper and sketch up my ideas before I even order the first packet of seeds. Coming up with a couple of rough drafts is a good way to get an idea of the number of plants you can grow without things getting out of hand.

Planting and preparing your plants for life outside

Young seedlings that have only known the windless warm world of life indoors can rarely handle direct transplanting into the garden soil. They usually require a two week period of hardening. Starting two weeks before your planned planting day you will want to put the plants outside each morning before you go to work and bring them inside each night before sundown.

If there is inclement weather or it is going to be unseasonably cold that day it is best to skip that day of hardening and leave the seedlings indoors. If you leave for work early and the temperature outside is 34 degrees or below, you should skip that day of hardening.

Another rule of thumb to follow is that seedlings should not be outside on a day when the forecasted high is 39 degrees or below. The physical properties of water begin to change at that temperature and this has the effect of poor nutrient up take in the plants roots.

Preparation is your best friend when it comes to preparing for planting day. Even though you might have waited for the average last frost date for your region, there is still a chance of a freak frost. Make sure you check the advanced forecast for any potential frost. Any time you see the overnight low forecasted for 36 degrees or colder you should plan on covering the plants.

Tilling the garden is about more than just making the ground soft enough for you to get a shovel into. It's also about providing soft soil for young roots to expand into as well as providing aeration. If you don't own a tiller and can't rent one, you can always use a spade shovel to spot till planting areas. When you spot till an area you want to loosen the soil in an area at least 2 feet in diameter and at least 18 inches deep per each plant.

When you plant the seedling remember the soil needs to be kept loose. Only a very light amount of hand tamping near the base of the plant is required to help seat it in the hole. If you are concerned about the wind blowing it over you can drive a small wooden stake into the soil and lightly tie the plants stem to it using cotton twine. Water the plant thoroughly once it is planted, preferably with warm water.

If you suffer the misfortune of having planted all of your vegetables and a freak frost threatens the garden you will have to cover the plants the night before. Remember the coldest time will be the hours just before dawn. Let the plant capture the warm part of the sun the day before and then cover a few hours before sunset.

Watering the plant, especially with warm water, will help protect the roots and allow the soil to help retain some heat energy overnight. When covering the plants an old sheet is a better insulator than a plastic tarp. Covering the plant with a 5 gallon bucket is also an option. Once, in a moment of desperation, when I had more plants in the ground than I had sheets and buckets, I did very well burying the plants inside mounds of fluffy straw. Admittedly, this made for a lot of work delicately removing the straw the next day.

Do not uncover the plants again until all threat of frost has passed. If there are back to back frost events in the forecast you can leave the plants covered for a full day and they will survive.

Each type of plant has its own unique needs through the course of a growing season. In the next section I will break each vegetable down to help you better understand how to grow it in the garden and cook with it in the kitchen.

Understanding Italian Cooking

For a lot of people when you discuss Italian cooking and Italian vegetables, it evokes images of rich marinara sauces, colorful peppers and a myriad of pastas topped with melted cheese. The truth is Italian cooking is really regionally inspired. What the average American thinks of as Italian Food is actually known as Neapolitan, from the area around Naples Italy.

The cuisine of northern Italy tends to use more fish and cured meats to pair with grains, potatoes, beans and stuffed pasta. Central Italy tends to use a lot of tomatoes and hot peppers, paired with a wide variety of meats and fish. Southern Italy still has a strong presence of tomatoes and peppers, with more emphasis on olives, olive oil, garlic, citrus, eggplants and zucchini.

It is a style of cooking so diverse and so tied into the sourcing of fresh ingredients that the best we can hope to do is dip a toe into the great sea of delicious dishes available while touching on vegetables you should be able to source from your American grocery store or garden.

Chapter 4 – Asparagus

Asparagus is actually one of the original Italian vegetables. The ancient Romans were snacking on fresh asparagus long before the discovery of the New World added beans, corn, potatoes and tomatoes to the menu.

In the garden, Asparagus is a perennial plant that can produce for over 20 years. It prefers sandy soil that allows it to send its roots deep. At the same time in peak season it prefers generous watering. It should be planted in a location that gives it at least eight hours of sunlight.

While you can grow asparagus from seed, it will require four years to establish itself enough to be harvested. You can find juvenile crowns available in early spring which will be mature enough to harvest by the third spring. Crowns are more productive sooner at only about twice the price and really are the best way to go.

Planting Asparagus

As soon as the soil in your garden is thawed, dig a hole two feet deep. Back fill the hole loosely with a foot of soil. Place the crown in the loose soil and spread the roots out. Apply a modest amount of a phosphorus rich fertilizer before watering. Then cover the crown loosely and mark the place where it was planted with a plant marker or stick.

The amount of time it takes for the shoots to emerge will vary depending on how warm the spring is and how long the crowns had been held in dormancy. In general you should expect to see the first little sprigs emerge in two weeks. If you haven't seen anything in four weeks then it probably means the crown did not survive. It's not outrageous for one to two crowns out of every ten to not make it.

Cultivating Asparagus

Cool soil temps will help asparagus as the spring heats up. Asparagus is also a heavy feeder so a nice dressing of rich compost or mature manure will fortify the plant once it emerges. Keep the soil well watered and well weeded.

Harvesting

Asparagus planted from crowns can be harvested on the third spring. Harvest spears that are roughly the thickness of your pinky finger, when they are six to seven inches tall. Using a sharp knife cut off the spears at the ground level. Wash the spears thoroughly before storing or cooking.

Cooking with Asparagus

Like many vegetables asparagus is best fresh. Immediately after being harvested asparagus starts the process of converting sugar compounds into starches. To prepare asparagus for cooking you will want to remove the woody end. Simply bend each individual spear, trim with a paring knife at the apex of the bend where the woody material meets the tender top.

Asparagus has a high concentration of antioxidants. It is also high in vitamin A, vitamin C, vitamin B6 and it has a high amount of dietary fiber.

Blanching asparagus for a minute in hot water is only needed if you have thick spears that have spent a lot of time in the refrigerator. Asparagus that is fresh from the garden can be cooked directly using a wide variety of high heat cooking methods.

Asparagus Featured Recipes

Italian style broiled asparagus

While this dish is meant to be a side dish that plays well with any red meat, it is also a great snack. This is a great alternative over a bag of chips for an evening snack!

Equipment

A half sheet pan lined with parchment paper

Silicone spatula

Medium size work bowl

Paper towel

Ingredients

1 Pound of fresh asparagus, trimmed

2 Tablespoons extra virgin olive oil

½ Teaspoon kosher salt

2 Cloves of garlic, minced

¼ Cup grated parmesan cheese

Procedure

Step 1: Wash and trim all asparagus. Pat dry with a paper towel and place in a medium work bowl.

Step 2: Adjust your oven rack to the highest position 4 to 6 inches below the broiler element. Then turn the broiler on its lowest setting.

Step 3: Slowly drizzle the olive oil over the asparagus, lightly tossing with a spatula. Once the Asparagus has been evenly coated by the oil add the minced garlic and kosher salt. Toss to evenly distribute.

Step 4: Spread the asparagus onto the baking sheet in a single layer. Place the baking sheet under the broiler element.

Step 5: After 4 minutes check the asparagus and shake the baking sheet to turn the spears for even cooking.

Step 6: After another 4 minutes the asparagus will be tender yet toothsome. Remove when the crowns begin to show browning.

Step 7: Plate the asparagus and sprinkle it with grated parmesan cheese.

Italian Asparagus Soup

This soup is best with young tender asparagus. It is also a great way to make use of the woody ends trimmed from asparagus spears.

Equipment

A medium stock pot

A medium sauce pot

Ingredients

1 Pound asparagus, trimmed

¼ Cup extra-virgin olive oil

4 Cloves of garlic minced

2 Cups red potatoes cut into quarters

2 Cups spring onions, chopped

4 Quarts chicken broth

1 Bay leaf

1 Tablespoon kosher salt

1 Cup Arborio rice

1 Cup Parmesan cheese, grated

½ Teaspoon fresh cracked black pepper

Procedure

Step 1: Pour one quart of chicken broth into a medium sauce pot on medium low heat.

Step 2: Wash and trim the asparagus spears. Then place the woody ends in the chicken broth. Simmer for 20 minutes.

Step 3: While the woody ends are simmering, cut the tender asparagus spears into one inch pieces.

Step 4: Pour ¼ cup of olive oil into a medium stock pot on medium low heat. Add the minced garlic and sweat for 2 minutes until it takes on a light color.

Step 5: Add the potato cubes in the hot oil. Stir until the potatoes start to stick to the bottom without browning. Approximately 4 to 5 minutes.

Step 6: Stir in the chopped spring onions.

Step 7: Remove from the heat for 1 minute.

Step 8: Remove the woody asparagus stalks from the chicken stock and discard. The stalks should have contributed some of their flavor to the broth.

Step 9: Slowly pour the asparagus infused chicken broth into the medium stock pot. Add the rest of the chicken broth and the bay leaf.

Step 10: Cook uncovered for 1 hour stirring occasionally. When the volume of the broth is reduced by half add the Arborio rice.

Step 11: Bring to a boil on high heat for 12-15 minutes until the rice is soft yet toothsome

Step 12: Season to taste with salt and fresh cracked black pepper. When plating, garnish each bowl with a heaping tablespoon of grated parmesan cheese. This soup is better paired with seasoned croutons rather than crackers.

Chapter 5 – Beans

There are actually many regional Italian dishes that call for beans as a featured ingredient. In the garden beans need to be trained. When companion planted with squash and corn the three plants benefit each other as the corn gives the beans a pole to grow up, while the beans deposit nitrogen in the soil and the squash provides shade to keep the soil moist.

There are two types of beans you can choose from; bush beans and pole beans. While both types of vines require training, the pole bean takes up less space. Beans are not a plant you want to start indoors. Once they germinate, beans have an aggressive growth trait which will have their tender roots balling up while their vines sprawl out of control.

Soil temperatures should be at a minimum of 60 degrees before planting. Cold soil delays germination and the high starch content of the bean seed when soaked in wet soil can cause the seed to rot rather than grow. If you make successive plantings of fresh beans two weeks and four weeks after the initial planting you will have multiple harvests of fresh beans through the season.

It is best to plant shell beans all at one time as the processing and storage later in the season can be tedious. Common types of shell beans range from Pinto to Kidney and of course Lima beans.

Green beans that are allowed to fully mature and dry on the vine become soup beans, sometimes called northern beans.

Italian culture is rife with scores of heirloom shell beans that are available in a myriad of colors, textures and flavor profiles.

Bean Featured Recipes

Tuscan White Bean Soup

This is an Italian classic soup that suspends cannellini beans in a vibrant flavorful broth. If you can't get your hands on cannellini beans you can substitute navy beans. Originally from Tuscany this soup has found its way around the world and even evolved to fit into other ethnic foods such as the Kale soup in Azorean cuisine.

Equipment

A large, enamel coated Dutch oven

Ingredients

2 Tablespoons extra-virgin olive oil

¼ Pound pancetta, or bacon, cut into 1 inch pieces.

1 Small red onion, chopped.

4 Cloves of garlic, minced.

¼ Teaspoon of fennel seeds

2 ½ Cups dried cannellini or navy beans, soaked overnight

8 Cups of chicken broth

1 Small bunch of kale, stemmed and chopped (Optional)

Salt and fresh cracked black pepper

Procedure

Step 1: Soak the beans in water over night.

Step 2: Add the bacon or pancetta to a large Dutch oven over medium-low heat. Once the meat begins to take on some browning, add the olive oil and onions, cook until the onions begin to look a little translucent.

Step 3: Add the garlic and fennel seeds. Cook for 2 minutes.

Step 4: Remove the pot from the heat for one minute before slowly adding the chicken broth.

Step 5: Return the pot to the heat and add the beans. Bring the pot to a boil.

Step 6: Cover and reduce heat and let simmer for 45 to 60 minutes or until beans are tender.

Step 7: If you prefer the addition of kale, add it to the soup and simmer for 7-10 minutes until the pieces of kale are wilted.

Step 8: Salt and pepper to taste.

This soup is best served with grilled bread or garlic toast instead of crackers. It is an excellent appetizer but also works easily as a main course that can warm your bones on a cold winter evening.

Sautéed Green Beans

I think for a lot of people the idea of green beans as a side dish evokes images of blanched over cooked string beans laying in a soggy heap on the side of your dinner plate. If you've spent your entire life eating canned green beans then I can understand a certain lack of enthusiasm for them. However Italian sautéed green beans might just change your mind.

Cooking them at high heat deepens the flavor profile. The use of aromatic vegetables and a squirt of lemon will enhance the fresh earthy flavors.

Equipment

Medium sauté pan

A Large pot of boiling water

Slotted spoon or spider strainer

Ingredients

2 Pounds of green beans with the ends trimmed

2 Tablespoons extra-virgin olive oil

2 Shallots, chopped fine

3 Cloves of garlic, minced

1 Teaspoon fresh lemon juice

Salt and fresh cracked black pepper to taste

Procedure

Step 1: Bring a large pot of water to a boil. Add the beans to the pot and blanch them for two minutes.

Step 2: Remove the beans from the water using a slotted spoon or spider strainer to a paper towel and pat them dry.

Step 3: Pour the olive oil into a medium sauté pan over medium heat. Add the shallots and garlic to the pan and sauté for two minutes.

Step 4: Add the green beans and increase the heat to medium-high. Sautee the beans for 4 to 5 minutes, tossing frequently, until the beans begin to take on some browning.

Step 5: Season with salt and fresh cracked black pepper to taste. Give the entire pan a light squirt of lemon juice just before plating.

This dish is a perfect side for roast pork or chicken. It is as much at home with a heap of mashed potatoes as it is alongside a mound of creamy Fettuccine Alfredo.

Chapter 6 – Eggplant

You might not think it, but eggplant is one of the most far traveled and diverse vegetables on the planet. It is originally from India. Picked up on the silk road headed east, it was transformed through seed selection into varieties like Ping Tung Long, Thai Long Green and Ma-Zu Purple. Middle Eastern people adapted the eggplant into Turkish Orange varieties.

Eggplant also found a loving home amongst the warm and fertile soils of Italy, Southern France and Spain. The common variety of eggplant you find in the grocery store is the Black Beauty. This is an eggplant that has shown traits for high productivity in the field, good handling at harvest and a long shelf life. While you can indeed do delicious things with Black Beauty it is not the most flavorful of the Southern European varieties.

In eggplants, the two things that work against you in regards to flavor are the skin's potential to develop bitterness and the development of seeds. The best heirloom varieties develop seeds late and have low bitterness in their skin. However, these two traits are usually opposed to creating a large bounty of fruit.

My top three heirloom suggestions if you are looking for a flavorful eggplant would be to go with, Rosa Bianca, Lista de Gandia or Rosita.

Rosita is actually a product of Puerto Rico through Spain. The skin is tender with little bitterness and the seeds develop late in the modest sized fruit. If you've never grown eggplant before or if you are new to cooking it, Rosita is probably your safest bet.

Lista de Gandia is visually striking with white and purple striations. It also makes a large fruit that has almost no bitterness in the skin. As an added bonus the plant is drought and blight resistant.

Rosa Bianca is hands down the most flavorful variety of eggplant I have ever found. The fruit is small, yet visually striking with its gossamer blends of purple and white. The plant is small and the yield is low. The saving grace of Rosa Bianca is not as much in the garden as it is in the kitchen, where it brings the most flavor combined with low water content to shorten prep time.

Eggplant is easy to start from seed, so long as you use a heated potting tray. Eggplant needs heat to germinate and loves warm soil temperatures the whole way through its lifecycle.

In the greenhouse the biggest concern is its surprisingly large leaves. On Monday it will be this cute little seedling with mouse ear leaves. By Wednesday night the leaves will have turned into catchers mitts blotting out the sun or choking out other seedlings from the grow lights. Since eggplant is one of the last things you will transplant into the garden it also means that it will have the time to grow huge in the greenhouse right at the time when everything else is fighting for space.

As a good rule of thumb you should allow a six inch radius around each eggplant and the seedlings next to it. You could reduce that size down to four inches if you're willing to rotate the seedling 90 degrees each day.

When planting time comes you want to remember that eggplants love warm soil temperatures. So don't even think of putting eggplant into the garden soil before other heat loving plants like squash, beans and corn.

Notes on cooking with Eggplant

Eggplant and Zucchini share the same foible in that they tend to have sponge like flesh that is a vehicle for other flavors. Because the porous flesh tends to hold onto a high water content if you don't attempt to dry them a little before cooking they can tend to get mushy.

Before cooking any eggplant dish you should allow a half an hour lead time to slice, salt and dry the eggplant.

Procedure for reducing eggplant water content

Adding a little bit of salt helps draw out the water, while the paper towel takes most of the salt and excess water away.

Step 1: Slice the eggplant to your desired thickness, usually one-quarter inch.

Step 2: Arrange the eggplant slices on a cutting board padded with a double layer of paper towel. Lightly salt both sides of each slice, then place them a single layer deep and cover them with another double layer of paper towel.

Step 3: Wait 15 minutes, then press down lightly on the top paper towel before flipping each piece.

Step 4: Lightly salt the top layer of the eggplant and replace the top with another double layer of paper towel.

Step 5: Wait another 15 minutes before lightly pressing on the eggplant slices.

They should now appear deflates in the middle with a mild beige hue in the center. They are now ready to cook.

Eggplant Featured Recipes

Caponata

Equipment

1 Large cook pot

1 Large serving bowl

Ingredients

4 Tablespoons olive oil

1 Large eggplant, unpeeled, salted and cut into 1 inch cubes

1 Large red onion, chopped

1 Medium red pepper, chopped

4 Large garlic cloves, minced

1 Pound diced plum tomatoes

2 Tablespoons fresh Basil, chopped

2 Tablespoons fresh oregano, chopped

2 Tablespoons fresh parsley, chopped

2 Tablespoons red wine vinegar

2 Tablespoons drained capers

Toasted pine nuts

Procedure

Step 1: Heat the oil in a large pot over medium-low heat. Add eggplant, onion and peppers. Sauté until the eggplant is soft and brown, about 10 minutes.

Step 2: Add the Garlic and sweat for two minutes.

Step 3: Add tomatoes, capers and herbs along with the red wine vinegar. Simmer for 10 minutes.

Step 4: Season to taste with salt and fresh cracked pepper.

Step 5: Plate the caponata in a large serving bowl. Sprinkle with toasted pine nuts and serve warm

Eggplant Parmesan

Eggplant Parmesan is a classic Italian comfort food. Even though there is no meat in this dish, it is still very hearty.

Marinara Sauce

Equipment

Medium sauce pot

Ladle

Ingredients

2 Pounds of diced plum tomatoes

1 Large yellow onion, chopped

4 Cloves of garlic, minced

8 Leaves of fresh basil, chopped

3 Tablespoons fresh oregano, chopped

Pinch salt

Pinch fresh ground black pepper

Pinch sugar

¼ Cup olive oil

Procedure

Step 1: Add olive oil to a medium sauce pot over a medium high heat. Allow a few minutes for the oil to come up to temp.

Step 2: Add the onions and sauté until they start becoming translucent. Add the garlic and sauté for one minute until golden.

Step 3: Add the tomatoes. Stir to combine and bring to a simmer.

Step 4: Add the basil, oregano, salt and pepper. Simmer on a low heat, stirring occasionally for 15 minutes.

Step 5: Taste the sauce, if it seems a bit green or bitter, add a pinch of sugar.

Eggplant Parmesan Preparation

Equipment

Dutch oven with 4 inches of peanut oil heated to 375

3 Large pie plates

Large work bowl

Draining rack

Paper towels

13x9 baking dish

Ingredients

1 Cup all-purpose flour

3 Cups Japanese bread crumbs

3 Large eggs, beaten

4 Cloves of garlic, minced

2 Tablespoons fresh oregano, chopped

1 Teaspoon fresh rosemary, chopped

2 Tablespoons fresh parsley, chopped and reserved for garnish

2 Pounds of eggplant cut sliced into half inch slices, salted and patted dry.

1 Pound mozzarella cheese

2 Cups of parmesan cheese

Salt and fresh cracked pepper to taste

Procedure

Step 1: Before starting the marinara sauce, slice, salt and press the water from the eggplant slices.

Step 2: While the salt is extracting water from the slices and the sauce simmers together, slowly heat the oil in the Dutch oven to 375 degrees.

Step 3: Preheat the oven to 375 degrees.

Step 4: Set up the pie plates where one has flour, the second has beaten eggs and the third has bread crumbs.

Step 5: Dredge the slices of eggplant first in the flour, then the egg and then the bread crumbs. Work in batches to keep it manageable.

Step 6: Slowly drop each slice into the hot oil and fry for 4-5 minutes or until they turn a medium brown.

Step 7: Remove the slices to a draining rack.

Step 8: Ladle a small amount of marinara sauce into the bottom of the 13X9 pan.

Step 9: Lay out a layer of breaded eggplant slices on the bottom of the pan. Then sprinkle with a layer of parmesan and mozzarella.

Step 10: Ladle a shallow amount of sauce over the cheese and repeat the layers again.

Step 11: Continue making layers of eggplant, cheeses and sauce until you are half an inch from the top lip of the pan. Then cover the top layer with the remaining cheese and garnish with chopped parsley.

Step 12: Place the pan in the oven uncovered and bake for 15-20 minutes or until the cheese is bubbling and turning golden brown at the edges.

Step 13: Remove from the oven and allow it to cool for 5-10 minutes before cutting pieces.

This dish is best when it follows a light appetizer salad tossed with a vinaigrette dressing. The brightness of the vinaigrette will wake up the palette and play well against the heaviness of the Eggplant Parmesan. Serve with medium red wine like Shiraz and soft fresh baked bread to help sop up the sauce.

Chapter 7 – Garlic

Garlic is a common ingredient in many Italian dishes. Its powerful aromatic presence adds fire and life to soups, pasta and meat dishes.

Garlic is planted by setting immature bulbs into the soil either in late fall or early spring. If you live in Growing Zone 5 or warmer you should plant garlic in early spring, as soon as you can till the soil. If you live in Growing Zone 4 or colder it is best to plant garlic in the late fall.

It is best to place the bulbs in the ground two to three weeks before the soil freezes. This will give the bulbs time to anchor their young roots before the soil hardens. With anchor roots they will be less likely to rise to the surface when the ground thaws in early spring.

Garlic absolutely must be planted in thoroughly drained, sandy soil. Soil that has a heavy clay content will restrict the bulbs greatly during the peak growing season and can potentially keep it from developing into a full cluster.

Garlic also prefers cool soil temps and like its sister the onion will bolt to seed rather than develop its root in warm soil. As such it should be planted on the south side of the garden or in a location that gets good morning sun and then partial to full shade in the afternoon.

As a member of the allium family, Garlic gets its magic from complex sulfur based flavor compounds. These sulfur compounds are volatile and start to break down when chopped and exposed to air or high heat. This means if you want a mellow garlic flavor in a dish you should put it in early. If you want garlic to have a powerful presence in a dish you should add it near the end.

Garlic Featured Recipes

Aioli

Technically Aioli is from Provence in southern France. Provence gets its name from the fact that it was the first province the Roman Empire annexed outside of the Alps. While aioli may have started in Provence it has none-the-less become a complimentary sauce in many other Mediterranean cultures. Aioli is the penultimate expression of the magic of garlic. No other sauce or dish allows garlic to shine brighter.

Real aioli is a sauce made from minced garlic married into an emulsion of eggs and olive oil. In Provence it is typically served as a sauce for salt cod or steamed vegetables. Just over the border in northern Italy it tends to be used with fresh seafood and potatoes.

There are a lot of ways to cheat at making an Aioli. The lowest end of the spectrum is to add garlic powder and lemon juice to a jar of mayonnaise. Some people will mince garlic and stir it aggressively into an olive oil mayonnaise to slide by.

Real aioli starts by grinding fresh garlic cloves with a mortar and pestle. This garlic paste is then slowly whisked together with a tender drizzle of olive oil incorporated with one egg yolk at a time. If you are concerned about the potential for salmonella with using uncooked egg yolks, you can always use pasteurized eggs.

Equipment

Mortar and pestle

Medium work bowl

Whisk

Ingredients

1 Cluster of garlic, approximately 10 large cloves

2 Large egg yolks

1 Teaspoon of mustard

1½ Cups of extra virgin olive oil

2 Tablespoons of fresh lemon juice

½ Teaspoon fresh cracked black pepper

Pinch of sea salt

Procedure

Step 1: A half hour before you plan to serve, separate the egg yolks and allow them to sit out in a covered bowl to come up to room temperature.

Step 2: While the egg yolks are coming up to room temperature, peel and crush the garlic. Then place the garlic in the mortar and pestle and grind them into a paste.

Step 3: Add the garlic paste, lemon juice, mustard and egg yolks to a medium work bowl. Whisk together slowly until they are thoroughly combined.

Step 4: Take a 2 minute rest. In the next stage of incorporating the olive oil you are going to need all of the arm strength that you can muster as you cannot stop whisking until all of the olive oil is combined!

Step 5: While continuously moving the whisk, very slowly drizzle in a small amount of olive oil. It takes time for the emulsion to get started so do not rush this stage. Adding the olive oil slowly and in very small amounts will make a strong emulsion that will last longer before eventually breaking.

Step 6: Once all of the olive oil is incorporated, season with a pinch of salt and fresh cracked black pepper.

You can store the Aioli in the refrigerator for up to four hours, but the longer it sits the greater the chance of it breaking.

Garlic Bread

Nothing goes better with a good plate of pasta than some fresh-from-the oven garlic bread. There are admittedly a lot of different ways you can make garlic bread. Some people are happy to butter a slice of toast and sprinkle garlic powder on it.

One of the more popular traditional methods is Crostini where garlic cloves are roasted in the oven and rubbed on a crust of bread. Another method is to infuse some quality extra virgin olive oil with minced garlic and then pinch off and dip fresh baked bread into the garlic oil.

At the end of the day there probably is no right or wrong way to make garlic bread. Instead think of this recipe as being my take on giving garlic bread all the bells and whistles.

Equipment

Half sheet pan

Fork

Small work bowl

Small sauté pan

Tinfoil

Ingredients

4 Cloves of garlic, whole

4 Tablespoons of butter at room temperature

2 Tablespoons extra virgin olive oil

1 Teaspoon of fresh chopped parsley

½ Teaspoon of fresh chopped rosemary

¼ Teaspoon fresh cracked black pepper

¼ Teaspoon lemon juice

Pinch of sea salt

Fresh baked Italian loaf of bread

Procedure

Step 1: Place the whole cloves of garlic, unpeeled, in a small sauté pan on medium low heat. When the skin on a clove gets a dark brown spot, rotate it. Once a clove has been through four rotations, remove it from the heat. The garlic should be soft enough after pan roasting that it will just squeeze out of the shell.

Step 2: Place the garlic in a small work bowl and mince it with the flat of a small fork.

Step 3: Add the butter, herbs, lemon juice, salt and pepper. Use the fork to blend together with the garlic.

Step 4: Slowly drizzle in the olive oil while blending with the fork.

Step 5: Preheat the oven to 400 degrees

Step 6: Cut the Italian loaf lengthwise and liberally apply the garlic-herb butter.

Step 7: Tent the top of each half loaf with tin foil.

Step 7: Place on a half sheet pan and toast in the oven for 5 minutes, then remove the tinfoil. Continue toasting until the edges of the bread are golden brown.

If you mix up the garlic herb butter a few hours before, the herb flavor will become more prominent while the garlic flavor will diminish. If you want to punch up the garlic more, simply pan roast more garlic, mince it and stir it in.

Chapter 8 – Peppers

Peppers are another new world vegetable that has found its way into the hearts and kitchens of many Italians.

Peppers are by their nature promiscuous pollinators and this means that they have transformed over the centuries into a myriad of different options. Italian cooking is not so much about spicy hot peppers like the Jalapeno or habanero. Instead Italian cooking tends to use bell peppers and seasoning peppers like the pepperoncini.

Peppers should be started from seed 8 to 10 weeks before the average last frost date for your region. Some peppers can take as long as four weeks to germinate if you don't use a heated potting tray. However with a heated potting tray you should expect they will germinate within 10-14 days.

After removing them from the heated potting tray you should pot the seedlings up in a larger pot, with the stem a half inch deeper in the new soil. After this you will never pot up the stem of the pepper again, unless you can see roots breaking the surface. If you see roots at the surface cover with another half inch of soil.

Since pepper plants love heat you should water them with warm water.

Plant them in the garden after they are well hardened, in a sunny location. The fruit of bell peppers can suffer from sun scald. It is best to feed peppers heavily with nitrogen early in the season in order to help them develop lush foliage. The large additional leaves will later help shade the tender peppers. Once they plants begin flowering, you should you a fertilizer that is high in soluble pot ash. This will help give the peppers more structure as they grow.

Peppers are generally mature when they ripen to red, however you can harvest most varieties when they are still green with only a minor loss of flavor.

Featured pepper recipes

Sausage and Peppers

Sausage and Peppers is one of the dishes that lost something in translation from Italy to America. I have been some places where it was treated more like a hot dog than a pan dish. This recipe is my Grandma's authentic take on Sausage and Peppers based on where she grew up near Naples.

Equipment

A large sauce pan

13X9 baking dish

Paring knife

Large sauce pan

Ingredients

12 Links or two pounds of Italian sausage

¼ Cup extra-virgin olive oil

10 Cloves of garlic, chopped

1 Pound of white button or Portobello mushrooms

2 Large yellow onions, julienned

6 Pepperoncini peppers, pickled or fresh, halved and seeded

1 Green bell pepper, seeded and cut into 1 inch strips

1 Yellow bell pepper, seeded and cut into 1 inch strips

1 Red bell pepper, seeded and cut into 1 inch strips

½ Cup of medium red wine

Procedure

Step 1: Using a paring knife, make three small holes on two sides of each sausage link.

Step 2: Drizzle some olive oil into the large sauce pan on medium heat and sear the sausages. Rotate each sausage so every side is lightly browned. Then remove the sausages to a 13X9 baking pan.

Step 3: Begin preheating the oven to 350 degrees.

Step 4: Place the mushrooms in the pan and sweat them for two minutes.

Step 5: Add all the peppers to the pan and sweat them for two more minutes.

Step 6: Add the onions to the pan and sweat them for two minutes.

Step 7: Add the Pepperoncini peppers to the pan.

Step 8: Add the garlic to the pan and sweat it for one minute.

Step 9: Pour the half cup of red wine into the pan and turn off the heat. Using a silicone spatula scrape some of the stuck on bits off the pan. Once the majority of the bits have deglazed into the wine, pour it over the sausages in the 13 X 9 pan.

Step 10: Toss all ingredients together and place the 13X9 Baking pan in the oven for 20-25 minutes. The dish is done when you can slice into a sausage link and it is cooked through with no pink.

This dish is best served family style with garlic bread and a medium red wine like Shiraz.

Peperonata

This dish can be used as a standalone vegetarian entrée. It also works great when paired with roasted chicken, leg of lamb or a grilled bone on pork chop.

Equipment

A large sauce pan

Ingredients

2 Cups of plum or cherry tomatoes, rough chopped

1 Green bell pepper, seeded and cut into 1 inch strips

1 Yellow bell pepper, seeded and cut into 1 inch strips

1 Red bell pepper, seeded and cut into 1 inch strips

1 Medium red onion, julienned

3 Tablespoons of Olive Oil

4 Cloves of garlic, minced

4 Pepperoncini peppers, pickled or fresh, halved and seeded

1 Teaspoon of red pepper flake

1 Tablespoon of fresh rosemary, chopped

1 Tablespoon of fresh oregano, chopped

1 Tablespoon of fresh basil, chopped

1 Teaspoon of thyme

1 Tablespoon of red wine vinegar

¼ Cup of a medium red wine

Salt and fresh cracked black pepper

Procedure

Step 1: Drizzle olive oil into a medium sauce pan on medium heat. Add the peppers and sauté for three minutes.

Step 2: Add the Onions and sauté for 3 to 5 more minutes or until the peppers begin to take on some color.

Step 3: Add the tomatoes, garlic, red wine and all the herbs except for the parsley. Reduce the heat to low.

Step 4: Simmer for 10-12 minutes or until most of the juices have cooked off.

Step 5: Salt and pepper to taste, then plate the peperonata with a garnish of chopped parsley.

This is a dish that is also delicious cold. It can be spooned on crostini or served alongside an omelet.

Chapter 9 – Potatoes

For some people, when they think of potatoes they think of Ireland or Idaho. In fact, since coming over from the New World the humble potato has found a home in the fertile soil of northern Italy. The mid altitudes and cool soil temperatures in the foothills of the Southern Alps are similar to the potatoes home range in the foothills of the Andes.

While there are a lot of options to choose from, like Kanabec and Yukon Gold, for most regional Italian dishes the options come down to Russet or Red Potatoes. Russet potatoes have brown skins and high starch content that breaks down. Russet potatoes most common use in American food is in mashed potatoes. Red potatoes, sometimes called waxy potatoes, hold their integrity better when cooked. In America red potatoes are commonly used in potato salad.

It's an easy temptation to look at the bag of potatoes in your pantry with eyes bulging and think about using them to plant in the garden. While you can plant them and some will grow, the number of plants that emerge will generally be less than half and the yield at the end of the season will be low. This is due to how the potatoes were processed in cold storage after harvest. Commercial growers will often spray potatoes with anti-sprouting agents in order to improve shelf life. Since the chemical permeates the skin it can't simply be washed off.

It is best to find a reputable dealer online or source quality seed potatoes from your local greenhouse supply. Potatoes need loose sandy soil in order to develop quality tubers. You should plant potatoes in the early spring 2-3 weeks after the ground thaws. As soon as the ground begins to thaw set your seed potatoes in a sunny window, the light will help spur the sprouting eyes to life.

You can cut potatoes into thirds or halves so long as there are at least two eyes per planting.

Till the soil thoroughly so it is as loose as possible. Plant each eye potato 6 to 8 inches deep. As the potatoes emerge continue to mound them up to the base of the lowest leaves with rich compost. Once the potatoes flower, stop mounding. Potatoes like to be properly watered but they do not want to be soaked or kept constantly wet. Instead it is best to choose a location that gets good morning sun and afternoon shade.

In midsummer red potatoes can be gently lifted with a hay fork and selectively harvested for baby red potatoes. After harvesting the medium sized red potatoes the plant should be lowered back down and thoroughly watered. If you intend to pull large potatoes from it in the fall then don't harvest the same plant twice in the summer

Russet potatoes do not do well if selectively harvested in this manner and young russets tend to have a green flavor to them.

Potatoes are technically in the same family as tomatoes and as such they are susceptible to the same pests and diseases. The two worst and most common are the Colorado potato beetle and the dreaded fungus known as early blight.

While insecticidal soaps will help with the Colorado potato beetle, I've found that the best solution is a light dusting of diatomaceous earth. Just be sure to reapply the powder after a heavy rain. If left unchecked the little red and black bugs will eat the leaves of the potato plant before laying their eggs. The larvae when they hatch are voracious eaters and will do even more damage to the plant and the stem than their parents.

Early blight is a leaf fungus that commonly affects tomatoes by wilting their leaves. While it travels on the wind it actually lives in the soil. As such you should never plant potatoes in an area where tomatoes grew the year before. Early blight begins as yellow and black spots on the lowest leaves of the plant and quickly begins to wilt and kill them as it moves on to younger leaves. If left unchecked it can potentially kill the plant by late summer and greatly reduce the final yield.

The best solution is to use a garden sprayer to apply organic copper sulfate. Spraying before the first signs of infection will make a huge difference through the season. As such I advocate spraying at the concentration advised on the label four weeks after planting and continuing the spray every 10 to 14 days depending on rainfall.

Follow the directions on the label in regards to timing the harvest before spraying that week.

Harvesting and storing potatoes

When harvesting the potatoes it is best to wait until the vines have died back at the end of the season. Lift all of the plant from the soil and pick the tubers from root mound. If you have had any problems with early blight in the season do not add the vines to your compost pile. It would be better to burn them.

Handle the potatoes as little as possible and do not wash them. They need time to cure and for the skins to dry. Store them in small batches in paper bags or burlap sacks in a cool, dry, dark place for two weeks. Washing them at all tends to leave water in the divot of the eyes where rot and bad spots can quickly form. For garden potatoes I leave the soil on them all winter long and only wash it off minutes before I plan to use them.

Featured Potato Recipes

Gnocchi

Gnocchi is a potato dumpling that plays a starch role like pasta for a variety of sauces ranging all across northern Italy. One of the biggest problems facing gnocchi is the dumplings turning out heavy. Nothing brings down the magic of a well prepared brown butter sauce like a gnocchi that hits the plate with a thud.

The more flour you use in the gnocchi the heavier and harder the dumplings will be. However, you need the flour to bring the gnocchi together properly, so it can't simply be left out. The water content of the potatoes is actually what dictates how much flour is needed when it comes time to roll out the dumplings. As such it is better to work with baked potatoes, rather than boiled or steamed.

Equipment

Half sheet pan

Potato ricer

Floured cutting board

Large work bowl

Fork

Large boiling pot full of water

Ingredients

4 Large russet potatoes, approximately two pounds

1 Cup all-purpose flour, reserved after flouring the board

1 Tablespoon salt

Procedure

Step 1: Poke holes in the potatoes and bake them for 45 minutes in a 350 degree oven, until completely soft.

Step 2: Using an oven mitt, remove the skins.

Step 3: Pass the potatoes through a ricer to thoroughly mash them without lumps. If there are any lumps in the potato mixture it will cause the gnocchi to break apart. Once the potatoes are riced and free of lumps place them in a large work bowl.

Step 4: Add ¾ of a cup of flour and the salt to potatoes. Use your hands to mix everything together. If the dough is still a little sticky, sprinkle some more flour into the bowl and knead it again. The goal is to use as little flour as possible.

Step 5: Roll the dough out into long ropes that are approximately ¾ of an inch thick. If the ropes break apart return the mixture to the bowl and sprinkle a little more flour and gently knead the dough again.

Step 6: Once the dough will roll out into a ¾ inch thick rope without breaking, use a dough scraper to chop the rope of dough into ¾" wide sections.

Step 7: Place each individual Gnocchi dumpling in the palm of your hand and roll it lightly with a fork to put grooves in it. While this can be very tedious, the grooves will help give the dumplings more surface area to adhere to.

Step 8: Allow 15 minutes for all the flour in each dumpling to properly hydrate.

Step 9: Fill a large boiling pot with at least one gallon of salted water and bring to a boil.

Step 10: Add the gnocchi to the boiling water in 2-3 medium sized batches. Allow each batch to cook for 3-4 minutes.

When it comes to saucing the gnocchi, a brown butter sauce with sage, parsley and parmesan is traditional. I have also seen people use Alfredo sauce with sautéed mushrooms.

In my family we prefer my Wife's Sage and gorgonzola cream sauce that I featured in Book III "Growing and Cooking Your Own Herbs." Since it is a family favorite, I have included it here as well.

Sage and gorgonzola cream sauce

Equipment

Medium sauce pot

Ingredients

1 Cup heavy cream

6 Ounces Gorgonzola cheese, cut into pieces

2 Tablespoons of butter

¼ Cup fresh sage leaves, chopped

2 Cloves of garlic, minced

1 Shallot, minced

½ Teaspoon fresh cracked black pepper

6 Baby Portobello or white button mushrooms, sliced and sautéed (optional)

Procedure

Step 1: In a medium sauce pot over low heat, melt the butter then sweat the garlic and shallots until they take on a little color. If you want to add optional mushrooms you should place them in the pan first and wait two minutes before adding garlic and shallots.

Step 2: Add the sage leaves and heavy cream to the pot and simmer. Stir frequently until cream is reduced in volume by half.

Step 3: Add the gorgonzola cheese in pieces. Stir until all the cheese melts and the sauce becomes smooth.

Step 4: Add the fresh cracked black pepper.

Step 5: Toss with the gnocchi or pasta of your choice.

This sauce is heavy so a white wine with brightness like a Riesling or Pinot Grigio will help cut the richness.

Herbed Baby Red Potatoes

Red potatoes are one of my favorite types of potatoes to grow in the garden because I can always raid a few of them in midsummer while still letting the rest of the plant grow until fall harvest. This herbed potato dish is a great side dish for any meat. It plays particularly well with lamb and chicken.

Equipment

A large sauce pan with a lid

A large serving bowl

Colander

Ingredients

2-3 Pounds of baby red potatoes, cleaned and cut into bite sized halves or quarters

3 Tablespoons of olive oil

1 Tablespoon of fresh oregano, chopped

1 Tablespoon of fresh rosemary, chopped

1 Tablespoon of fresh basil, chopped

2 Tablespoons of fresh parsley, chopped

2 Tablespoons of fresh squeezed lemon juice

1 Small red onion, chopped fine

2 Cloves of garlic, minced

¼ Cup of parmesan cheese, shaved

Salt and fresh cracked black pepper

Procedure

Step 1: Add the potatoes to a large sauce pan and pour in one inch of lightly salted water. Bring to a boil, then lid and reduce heat to low. Simmer for 15-20 minutes until potatoes are tender when pierced with a fork.

Step 2: Pour off any excess water and reserve the potatoes in a colander.

Step 3: Pour the olive oil in the pan, increase heat to medium-low. Add the onions and garlic. Sweat them for 2-3 minutes or until the onions start to look translucent.

Step 4: Add the potatoes, herbs, salt and black pepper. Give the pan a splash of lemon juice to help cut any heaviness from the olive oil. Toss to combine and heat through for 2-3 minutes.

Step 5: Spoon the entire contents of the pan into a serving bowl and cover with shaved parmesan.

The parmesan cheese should melt quickly with the residual heat of the potatoes. This dish is best served family style. However if you plate it individually it is best to hold on the parmesan cheese until after you have plated.

Chapter 10 – Tomatoes

Tomatoes are the star of the summer garden. The offerings in the grocery store cannot hold a candle to the depth of flavor offered by garden fresh tomatoes. At the same time, tomatoes are one of the most diverse heirloom vegetables.

Tomatoes come in determinate and indeterminate varieties. A determinate tomato has a trait that causes it to ripen fruit all at once. This is great if you are looking to spend a weekend doing a massive canning session to put up tomatoes for the winter. If, however, you are interested in spreading your tomato harvest out over the long growing season, then indeterminate varieties are better. The fruit of indeterminate tomatoes ripen at staggered intervals through the season. However, the shorter the days get as summer moves towards fall, the faster the tomatoes will start to ripen.

Most home gardeners prefer to grow indeterminate plants to give them a long and full season of tomatoes.

There are essentially three different types of fruit: Slicer tomatoes, cherry tomatoes and plum tomatoes.

Slicer tomatoes are the iconic big red globe often cut thin for salads and sandwiches. From a culinary stand point they are actually the least versatile. Their high water can make for thin sauces, while their relatively low sugar content puts them behind cherry tomatoes for snacking out of hand.

Cherry tomatoes are often thought of for their role in salads and eating out of hand. However, Cherry tomatoes have a unique sweetness that lends itself to other culinary roles, chopped into chutney or even sautéed as a side dish.

Plum tomatoes are by far the most useful tomato from a culinary standpoint. They can be roasted, made into sauces or stewed, and are the best tomatoes for canning. Of the forty tomato plants I grow each year twenty-five of them are plum tomatoes.

Tomatoes are easy to grow from seed with a heated potting tray and grow lights. They should be started 8 to 10 weeks before the average last frost date for your area. Shortly after germinating the seedling should be potted up into a larger pot. Since tomatoes are technically a vine the stem can be buried deeper and new roots will sprout from the buried section of the plant.

If the seedlings develop a purple hue under the leaves it is a sign of low phosphorus in the soil. You can easily fix this by mixing a phosphorus rich fertilizer at half strength. If you notice a yellow in the leaves in between green veins it is a sign of a mineral deficiency, usually due to over watering. You should skip the next watering, then fertilize with water dissolved with Epsom salt.

When you plant the tomatoes in the garden it is best to bury them to just below the bottom of the lowest leaves. Then mulch with an inch of straw to reduce the chance that watering and rain will spatter soil onto the plants leaves.

Tomatoes are very susceptible to the leaf fungus early blight. While it travels on the wind early blight actually lives in the soil. As such, you should never plant tomatoes in an area where potatoes grew the year before. Early blight begins as yellow and black spots on the lowest leaves of the plant and quickly begins to wilt and kill them as it moves on to younger leaves. If left unchecked it can potentially kill the plant by late summer and greatly reduce the final yield.

As for potatoes, the best solution is to use a garden sprayer to apply organic copper sulfate. Spraying before the first signs of infection will make a huge difference through the season. I advocate spraying at the concentration advised on the label four weeks after planting and continuing the spray every 10 to 14 days depending on rainfall.

Follow the directions on the label in regards to timing the harvest before spraying that week.

Harvest

Harvesting tomatoes is one of the great joys of summer. A vine ripened tomato is a very rare thing. Most of what the grocery store offers are actually picked semi-ripe then sprayed with ethylene gas which causes a chemical compound in the flesh of the green-orange tomato to turn red. However the flavor compounds remain immature and the flavorless starches have not converted to sugars. In short the grocery store is offering you a green tomato that a trick of science has managed to turn red.

A truly ripe tomato hanging from your garden vine is a truly delicate thing. Since the starch compounds have converted to water laden sugars the flesh is soft. Each type of tomato wants to be picked in a certain way.

A ripe cherry tomato releases from the vine easily and can be hand plucked. A plum tomato often needs to be pinched by the green and twisted. A large slicer tomato can sometimes be so soft and juicy that if you simply grab and pull you could damage the tomato. The safest way to pick a large slicer tomato is to use a small garden or kitchen shears and snip the stem right where it meets the greens of the tomato.

Vine ripened tomatoes keep best when they are kept cold. When canning tomatoes it is best to blanch whole tomatoes and remove the skins.

Procedure for Canning Tomatoes

Step 1: Wash tomato and remove the greens.

Step 2: Use a paring knife to make an X in the skin on the blossom end of the tomato.

Step 3: Drop the tomato into a pot of boiling water and allow it to simmer for 2 to 3 minutes.

Step 4: Remove the tomato from the boiling water and place in an ice bath. This shocking and cooling will help split the skin and loosen it from the meat.

Step 5: Peel the skin from the tomato and you can use the tomato immediately or place it in a quart sized canning jar to be put up.

Step 6: Fill all canning jars with tomatoes after adding "two tablespoons of bottled lemon juice or 1/2 teaspoon of citric acid per quart of tomatoes" to follow USDA acidity recommendations.

Step 7: Top with new lids and properly washed rings.

Step 8: Place the jars in a stock pot of boiling water so that they are covered by 2 inches of water. Boil for 15 minutes and remove.

Step 9: Allow the jars to cool and make sure all lids have popped down before storing.

Store the jars in a cool, dry, dark place for up to two years.

Tomato Featured Recipes

Ragu

When I was a boy this was a Sunday staple of Grandma's kitchen. Every Sunday she made what she called "Gravy" or what some people might call a marinara sauce. Traditionally it is a thick sauce made from slow cooked tomatoes and stewed meat. Once the meat is braised in the tomato base it is removed and served as a first course. The tomato sauce is then tossed with textured pasta as the second course mopped up with soft, absorbent bread known as Scarpetta.

Over the years I have made some admittedly Americanized changes to the recipe while still remaining true to the heart and soul of the dish. The red wine in this recipe is optional, yet serves a purpose in that there are some flavor compounds in tomatoes that are alcohol soluble. The wine unlocks these flavor compounds releasing them into the sauce as the slow cooking heat evaporates the alcohol.

Equipment

A medium stock pot

Food Processor

Paring knife

Ingredients

5 Pounds of plum tomatoes, diced

2 Pounds of Italian sausage links

2 Large yellow onions, chopped

1 Green bell pepper, chopped

1 Cup of Kalamata olives, chopped

1 Cluster of garlic, approximately 12 cloves, minced

¼ Cup of olive oil

1 Cup of medium red wine

1 Tablespoon of beef bouillon

½ Cup of fresh basil, chopped

½ Cup of fresh oregano, chopped

¼ Cup of fresh rosemary, chopped

2 Tablespoons of fresh thyme

Salt and fresh cracked black pepper

1 pound of textured pasta, rotini or rigatoni

Procedure

Step 1: Make 3 small slashes in each side of the sausages with a paring knife.

Step 2: Drizzle a little olive oil in a medium stock pot on medium heat. Then add the sausages and sear until they are brown on all sides.

Step 3: Dice the tomatoes in a food processor while the sausages sear.

Step 4: Add the chopped onions and one cup of tomatoes to the pot. Allow the tomatoes and onions to sear until the onions begin to take on a little color. Searing a small amount of the tomatoes will unlock additional depth of flavor in the final dish.

Step 5: Add the rest of the tomatoes, peppers, beef bouillon and red wine. Reduce the heat to low and allow them to simmer together for two hours.

Step 6: Add the chopped Kalamata olives and herbs, stir to incorporate and simmer for another 2-3 hours

Step 7: Boil one gallon of water in a large cook pot. Add one pound of textured pasta like rotini or rigatoni. Cook the pasta until it is al dente. Drain the pasta and incorporate it into the ragu and allow the pasta to finish in the sauce. This will help saturate the sauce into the contours of the pasta.

Step 8: Plate family style with the sausages served on the side.

Shaved parmesan and chopped parsley make an excellent garnish. This meal is not complete without fresh baked bread to sop up the remaining sauce on the plate. Pair with a red wine like Shiraz.

Sautéed Cherry Tomatoes

Equipment

Medium sauté pan

Ingredients

2 Cups of cherry tomatoes, halved

2 Tablespoons of olive oil

2 Cloves of garlic, minced

¼ Small red onion, sliced thin

1 Pepperoncini pepper, chopped

1 Tablespoon fresh basil, chopped

1 Tablespoon fresh oregano, chopped

1 Tablespoon fresh parsley, chopped

½ Teaspoon coarse ground salt

½ Teaspoon fresh cracked black pepper

2 Tablespoons medium red wine

Procedure

Step 1: Halve the cherry tomatoes.

Step 2: Heat the oil in a medium sauté pan over medium heat. Then add the onion and sauté for 1 minute.

Step 3: Add the Garlic and pepperoncini pepper and sauté for 1 minute.

Step 4: Add the halved tomatoes and salt. Sauté for 3 minutes tossing frequently.

Step 5: Remove the pan from the heat, add the red wine, oregano, basil and rosemary. Then return to the heat and sauté for 2 more minutes.

Step 6: Add the fresh cracked black pepper and garnish with fresh parsley.

This dish is great served alongside grilled white meats like pork and chicken. It is also a great side dish for a breakfast omelet or a frittata.

Tomato and Mozzarella Salad

This salad is a simple preparation that will allow you to make the most of excess slicer tomatoes. It is important to make sure the slicer tomatoes are thoroughly chilled.

Ingredients

2 Large ripe slicer tomatoes, sliced thin

¼ Cup of fresh basil, chiffonade

1 Tablespoon fresh oregano, chopped

½ Red onion, sliced thin

2 Cups of romaine lettuce, chopped rough

3 Tablespoons extra-virgin olive oil

3 Tablespoons quality balsamic vinegar

8 ounces of fresh mozzarella, sliced

Salt and fresh cracked black pepper

Procedure

Step 1: Slice the fresh mozzarella and pat dry any excess moisture.

Step 2: Arrange a bed of chopped romaine on the plate.

Step 3: Slice the tomatoes thin and arrange the slices alternating with the mozzarella.

Step 4: Sprinkle the onion, herbs, salt and pepper over the entire dish.

Step 5: Drizzle the oil and balsamic vinegar over the dish. Serve immediately.

This dish is an excellent appetizer or, when served with warm bread, can stand alone as a light lunch

Chapter 11 – Zucchini

Zucchini is a summer squash in the same family with crookneck and pattypan squash. Zucchini grows quickly and can get root bound easily so you should only start it indoors two weeks before you intend to plant it. The roots of zucchini are very tender and prone to transplant shock. When potting it up you should always choose a peat pot or newspaper pot that will allow the roots to easily grow through it.

Zucchini loves warm soil and should not be planted until soil temperatures are at least 65 to 70 degrees. Zucchini does best in full sun but its vines and fruit require frequent watering so be sure to mulch with a layer of compost and straw.

Some types of zucchini have a vining trait that will allow you to grow them on a trellis. This is a great way to save space in the garden. Just make sure the trellis is at an angle roughly equal to your degree of latitude on the globe. If you are intending to grow zucchini to a large size for shredding or baking you will want to make a sling for large fruit to keep them from breaking off the vine.

Costa Romanesca is a very flavorful heirloom variety that is growing in popularity and is a great choice for the garden and kitchen.

For most culinary uses zucchini are best when you pick them small. The ideal zucchini for cooking should be picked at no more than 6 to 8 inches long. You can also harvest zucchini blossoms for stuffing or deep frying. You should only select male blossoms which can be identified by their long stem inside the flower. Also female blossoms have a bulge at the base where the flower meets the stem of the plant. This bulge is where the actual zucchini will form.

Cooking with Zucchini

Zucchini and Eggplant share the same foible in that they tend to have sponge like flesh that is more of a vehicle for other flavors. Because the porous flesh tends to hold onto a high water content if you don't attempt to dry them a little before cooking they can tend to get mushy.

Before cooking any zucchini dish, you should allow a 15 minutes lead time to slice, salt and dry the zucchini.

Procedure for reducing zucchini water content

Adding a little bit of salt helps draw out the water, while the paper towel takes most of the salt and excess water away.

Step 1: Slice the zucchini to your desired thickness, usually one-quarter inch.

Step 2: Array the zucchini slices on a cutting board padded with a double layer of paper towel. Lightly salt both sides of each slice before placing them a single layer deep and covering with another double layer of paper towel.

Step 3: Wait 7 minutes, then press down lightly on the top paper towel before flipping each piece.

Step 4: Lightly salt the top layer of the zucchini and replace the top with another double layer of paper towel.

Step 5: Wait another 7-8 minutes before lightly pressing on the zucchini slices.

They should now appear deflated in the middle with a mild yellow tint in the center.

Zucchini Featured Recipes

Deep Fried Zucchini Blossoms

A quick frying crisp tempura batter is better for frying male zucchini blossoms than say a cornmeal or seasoned flour dredge.

Equipment

A deep fryer or enamel coated Dutch oven

Fry thermometer

Draining rack

Paper towels

Large work bowl

Pie plate or small shallow work bowl

Blender

Ingredients

Enough peanut oil to fill the Dutch oven 4 inches deep or fill deep fryer to manufactures specifications

2 Cups of all-purpose flour

½ Cup of cornstarch

4 Egg yolks

1 ½ Cups of seltzer water

1 Teaspoon salt

Pinch of garlic powder (Optional)

8-10 Fresh picked male zucchini blossoms

Procedure

Step 1: Begin heating the oil to 370 degrees.

Step 2: Add the egg yolks and seltzer water to a blender and pulse to combine.

Step 3: Add the flour and salt and blend until smooth. Then pour the batter into a large work bowl.

Step 4: Evenly spread the cornstarch in a pie plate or shallow work bowl.

Step 5: Dredge each zucchini blossom in the cornstarch. Shake off any excess before dipping it in the large work bowl with the tempura batter.

Step 6: Slowly place the blossom in the hot oil. Fry for 3 to 4 minutes or until golden brown. Do not fry more than 3-4 blossoms at a time.

Step 7: Remove the blossom from the oil and onto a draining rack lined with a paper towel.

Some people prefer a dipping sauce of seasoned sour cream or even thousand-island dressing with their deep fried zucchini blossoms. Personally I like to give them a squirt of lemon, a sprinkle of fresh cracked black pepper and then serve them on the side of a pasta dish with a rich marinara sauce.

Stuffed Zucchini

Stuffed zucchini in America tends to be a fair food where a whole zucchini is cored out and stuffed with meat and cheese before being breaded and deep fried.

The stuffed zucchini I know and love is made by splitting young tender zucchini, carving out the seed cavity then mounding it with seasoned rice and melted parmesan cheese.

This is one of my favorite side dishes for summer time grilling. However if you don't have a grill you can do the same thing with a conventional oven.

Equipment

Teaspoon

Grill or oven

2 Quart sauce pot

Ingredients

1 Tablespoon olive oil

1 Teaspoon fresh oregano, chopped

1 Teaspoon fresh parsley, chopped

½ Cup white basmati rice

1 Cup water

½ Teaspoon salt

Fresh cracked black pepper

2 Cloves of garlic, minced

½ Small red onion, chopped

½ Cup cherry tomatoes, chopped

¼ Cup of parmesan cheese, minced

Squirt of fresh lemon juice

2 Young zucchini, approximately 8 inches long

Procedure

Step 1: In a 2-quart heavy saucepan, heat oil over low heat. Add rice and stir for 1 minute.

Step 2: Add water, lemon juice, and salt, bring to a full boil.

Step 3: Once it is boiling add garlic, onion, and oregano. Reduce to low heat, cover and simmer for 20 minutes.

Step 4: Start your grill or preheat your oven to 350 degrees.

Step 5: Cut the zucchini the long way. Then use a teaspoon to carve out the seed core of each zucchini half. You should take enough of the seed core that you leave behind a smooth surface of meat.

Step 6: Once you have the pocket carved out coat it liberally with salt. Then turn it upside down over a paper towel.

Step 7: Once the rice has absorbed all of the water add the chopped tomato and toss the mixture with a fork. The residual heat of the rice should warm the tomato chunks. Place the lid on the pot to hold some of the heat but keep the stove top off.

Step 8: Take the zucchini halves and press the cavity with a dry paper towel to extract any additional moisture.

Step 9: Lightly drizzle olive oil on the zucchini and place them face down on the grill grates over direct heat or face down on a pan in the oven. Cook face down for 7-10 minutes, until the face of the zucchini starts to soften a little.

Step 10: Turn the zucchini over and mound the rice into the cavity. Sprinkle with fresh cracked black pepper.

Step 11: Bake for 5-7 minutes or until the thickest part of the zucchini near the blossom end feels soft when poked with a toothpick.

Step 12: Remove from the oven and cover with shaved parmesan cheese and a garnish of chopped fresh parsley.

This dish works and plays well with grilled chicken and fish. Serving it with a bright white wine like Riesling will help bring out some of the citrus notes infused in the rice.

Conclusion

Learning to grow my own vegetables to cook the Italian dishes of my childhood has been a lifelong adventure. For me it is a lifestyle choice that has allowed me to reconnect with my past while providing delicious home grown and scratch made meals for my family every day. It is a passion that is in my blood which drives me forward to keep learning from my mistakes and growing as much on the inside as I do on the outside.

If you're new to the world of gardening or you are a proficient gardener who wants to become a better home cook it is easy enough to pick a few vegetables and a handful of dishes to get you started. With a little learning along the way this hobby can become an obsession that changes the way you look at your life and the way that you feed the ones you love.

Part III - Growing and Cooking Your Own Herbs

A Quick Start Guide to Growing and Cooking Popular Herbs from Basil and Cilantro to Rosemary and Sage

Introduction

Publishers Note: The introduction and a few of the growing instructions in Part III are similar to sections of Part II with variations when it comes to the specific mention of herbs. The full text has been included here to maintain the integrity of the original book. The rest of the information in Part III is specifically about growing and cooking herbs and therefore is different than Part II.

When I was a child my mother worked a lot of double shifts. While she was slaving away in a hot factory I was looked after by the elderly Italian woman who lived next door. She and her husband were immigrants who came to America after World War Two. They spent most of their adult lives running an Italian restaurant. They retired to the house next door just a few weeks before I was born.

Since my own Grandparents had passed away years earlier, I came to call them Grandma and Papa. While the blood on both sides of my family is German, my childhood in Grandma's kitchen gave me an Italian soul.

Each morning she would take me to the garden. I would follow along at her side as she tended to an immense assortment of herbs, tomatoes and peppers. As she weaved from row to row was always my job to hold the picking basket. She always started in the tomatoes, before picking her way through ripe peppers and finishing up in the verdant maze of fresh herbs.

I have wonderful memories of her laying fresh basil and rosemary top of a mound of crimson red, vine ripened tomatoes. She would then take my hand and we would walk back to the house. She would wash everything while I sat on the floor smelling the aroma of fresh herbs that had transferred from her hand to mine.

She sang classic Italian songs as she washed the vegetables. I never understood the lyrics but they were none-the-less a lullaby soothing me down for my morning nap. As soon as she was done washing everything she would scoop me up and lay me down in my day bed. She would finish the last song and I would put my herb scented hand near my face.

To this day the smell of rosemary and basil reminds me that I was loved.

I would get up from my nap an hour later and lunch was served. Steam bowls of fresh pasta enrobed in rich aromatic sauces, dressed with cheeses and fresh herbs. I would devour meatballs the size of my head and sop up red sauce with fluffy hunks of scarpetta bread.

Many people talk of their childhood memories with evocative descriptions of chocolate chip cookies, chicken noodle and Technicolor sugary cereals. For me it was those memories of scratch made Italian classics.

Unfortunately Grandma and Papa died shortly before my 9th birthday. Daily meals of scratch made Italian classics, fresh baked bread and aromatic herbs was ripped from my life. It was replaced by a soul rending menu that mostly consisted of cans of ravioli, frozen pizza and grainy microwave hamburgers.

I have spent years of trial and error in the kitchen, guided only by my memories as I learned to recreate her cooking. I found very quickly that the difference between dried herbs and fresh is night and day. This meant if I was going to create the magic of her spicy aromatic pesto sauce, I was going to have to learn to grow basil. If I was going to ever going to sink my teeth into the soft fluff of rosemary focaccia bread, then I was going to have to tend a rosemary bush.

One of the things that makes Italian cooking such a favorite at so many restaurant and kitchen tables is that to really do it right you have to use the freshest and best ingredients. You honor those ingredients by preparing them with care. The end result is a dish where everyone at your table can taste the love.

This is a product of putting in the time to learn how to grow and cultivate vegetables and herbs or find them at farmer's markets and grocery stores. Sure, you can get these things from a jarred sauce or a freezer case box of something but it's going to be the cooking equivalent of ending a hot date with handshake instead of a long kiss goodnight.

Even if you are not interested in Italian cooking, these basic herbs translate into many other recipes and types of cuisine. A few of the recipes I have included in this section are from other areas of the world.

The information that follows is from my own experience and research. It's worth noting that I am not some master chef who studied in Naples. I am not hocking my knowledge to become the next celebrity chef with a cooking show and a spiffy catch phrase.

I am essentially just like you. I work a daily grind, I try to raise my daughter right, I work on the side as a freelance writer and I cook almost all of the meals my family eats from scratch.

Chapter 1 – Choosing the right equipment

I admit that developing a green thumb is to a home gardener what finding your voice is to an aspiring writer. It doesn't always come easy, it might take a little more forethought than you expect and you're going to have to learn from your mistakes along the way.

Some herbs are easy to start from seed. Others can feel like a total crapshoot before you find success. With oregano you simply scatter seeds on dirt, make it wet and put it in a sunny window. Rosemary I was only able to germinate and nurture one good plant out of twenty five seed plugs.

On a practical level some herbs are just easier to buy from the nursery rather than spend countless attempts trying to grow from seed. Later when we get to the specific herb entries I'll include notes on sourcing seeds versus plants.

This chapter will focus on the basic set up you will need to start herbs from seed indoors.

While each type of herb might have its own special needs through the course of the season, most will germinate with a little heat, water, light and peat moss.

Seed Starting Kits

A lot of stores these days begin offering seed starter kits sometimes called heated miniature greenhouses, or heated potting trays, as early as January.

The kit comes with an electric warming mat, resting in a protective base tray. Sitting on top of the heat mat is a domed potting tray full of small rehydrated peat moss seed plugs. When the peat moss plugs are properly hydrated and the warming mat is plugged in it supplies a gentle heat to the soil.

The constant heat supply is set around 72 to 75 degrees. The removable domed top of the potting tray keeps moisture from evaporating away. When you set the unit under grow lights or the sunlight from a window with a southern exposure, the seeds will in optimal conditions for germination.

Most of the time when you buy the kit it is an all in one package that is already filled with dehydrated peat moss seed plugs in it. Every year you can buy new plugs and reuse the rest of the kit. Just speaking from my own experience they generally start to lose a little something in the heating element after six years of heavy use.

Different annual herbs may have different start times before the season. So make sure you know how soon to start the seeds before the average last frost date for your region. If you don't know the average last frost date for your area, you can usually find it by contacting or searching your state's agricultural extension office. Since most herbs will not tolerate even a light frost on their delicate leaves you want to make sure plants will not be subject to frost. At the same time root bound plants can hurt the long term production during peak season.

Location

While it's true that you could stick your potting tray and grow lights in any old basement closet and have modest success. There are a few factors to consider that will improve your chances of having strong healthy plants for your summer time garden.

Once seedlings germinate they will crave light. Even a strong grow light placed too high overhead will encourage a plant to grow its stem too long, become leggy and fall over. So you will want a location that allows you to adjust the height of your grow lights so that the bulbs are always two to four inches above the highest leaves of the plant.

You also want to have an area available outside of the heated potting tray. While some herbs crave bottom heat on their roots and will thrive, others will begin to get leggy if heat is kept in the soil plug for more than a day or two after germination.

For non-heat loving herbs you will want to remove them from the potting tray within 24 hours of germinating and pot them up into whatever seedling pot you have chosen for them to grow in until it is time for them to be transplanted into the garden.

I have a 24 inch by 48 inch wire bakers rack with adjustable shelves that I use every spring for potting up seedlings. The wire shelves allow me to hook things on, adjust chains or store all the little odds and ends I need without cluttering up the main potting shelf.

Choosing, installing and using grow lights

These days there are a lot of options you can choose from when it comes to grow lights. There is more than enough science behind it to give you a nose bleed.

Here is a quick summary of your available options and what you need to know.

Plasma: This is a new form of grow light technology. It claims to have the best efficiency and best spectrum of light. From my initial research into the cost, energy usage and the amount of area a single average light can cover, this appears to be more of a commercial grow light.

LED: When LED grow lights first appeared in the marketplace a lot of technical promises were made that ultimately under delivered. While the technology, spectrum range and efficiency has improved rapidly in recent years LED lights can still be a pretty large upfront investment for something as simple as starting seedlings indoors.

High Intensity Discharge: This is probably the most common type of grow light. It is efficient and comes in two different options, Metal Halide and High Pressure Sodium. For starting seedlings and over wintering herbs indoors you will want the Metal Halide Bulbs, which cast towards the blue end of the spectrum. High Pressure Sodium Lights tend to cast in the yellow end of the spectrum meant to mimic waning light of the fall season, which triggers flowering and fruiting plants to bloom. High pressure sodium lights tend to be used by people who grow vegetables indoors all year long.

Fluorescent: This is by far the cheapest and easiest of your grow light options. You will want to buy Full spectrum daylight bulbs, which cost around $10 each and from my experience they have an average lifespan of six years. Any standard 48 inch shop light fixture will hold the bulbs and costs between $15 and $20.The bulbs and the fixtures commonly go on sale in a lot of hardware stores in early February.

Personally I have been using a four fixture Fluorescent grow light system that I cobbled together years ago for $60. In the last seven years I have lost one fixture and one bulb, as a result of a spill while watering.

Window Box: In the spring of 2005 I planted more aggressively than my grow light space allowed. As a result I was forced to start and grow forty plants in a window with a great southern exposure. I can tell you from personal experience that it is possible to start and grow strong plants for a few weeks in a sunny window. In fact only two plants died in the window box before planting day.

It is obviously the cheapest option available to you if you have a window with a good southern exposure. Ironically it is also the most labor intensive. Since young seedlings crave light, they will bend and reach for the strongest light source. If you don't rotate each seedling at least once per day it will cause them to reach too far and become leggy. A leggy plant can easily die if allowed to lean for too long. Even if it survives the weak stem can struggle against strong summer winds in the garden.

Placing a dozen or so plants on small trays or old cookie sheets is a fast option for rotating the plants.

If you do not have a window with a strong southern exposure you can get by with an eastern exposure. Seedlings will be most hungry for light in the morning. A pure western exposure encourages legging.

Chapter 2 – Get ready, set grow

Preparing and planting your seed plugs

Once you've established where you want to keep your seed tray you will need to rehydrate the seed plugs. The seed plugs start out as little coins of peat moss that you have to soak in water and they will expand for planting.

There are essentially two different types of soil plugs you can choose from, netted or non-netted. I always choose the netted kind, which comes wrapped in a small mesh that expands when the plug is rehydrated. The fine holes expand easily for the roots to escape when the seedling is potted up to a larger planter. The non-netted kind can sometimes flake apart as the roots expand or can get wedged the in the tray and break off when you pull them out.

Usually the instructions that come with the kit tell you place the dehydrated peat moss coins into little slots and fill the tray with warm water. The peat moss coins will slowly expand into soil plugs that are held in place by the plastic slots. I've personally found that this can be a problem since sometimes the soil plugs don't absorb all of the water in the tray. It can be a real pain to try to pour away or bail out the excess water.

What I prefer is to use a small pale or ice cream bucket filled with warm water. I put the exact number of dried plugs into in the water for the type of herb I am planting I'm planting at that time. Then I plant using the following procedure.

Step 1: The plugs will take five minutes to rehydrate. While they are expanding in the water, open your seed packet and dole out two to three times the number of seeds onto a sheet of white paper. I always plant at least double the number of seeds in case of germination failure. If all of them germinate I will later cull or remove the weaker plant by snipping it off where the root meets the stem.

Step 2: When the seed plugs are expanded place them in their spot in the potting tray. If you chose the mesh wrapped style of plugs gently use your fingers to fully open the mesh on top. Then use a tooth pick to rough up the top quarter inch of peat moss.

Step 3: Carefully place the seeds into peat moss and lightly sink them into the plug. The general rule of thumb is to plant the seed three times deeper than the diameter of the seed. Rarely will you exceed a quarter of an inch.

Repeat these steps for each type of herb you are planting. Then cover the potting tray with the clear plastic dome and plug in the heat mat.

While the germination time for each type of herb can vary, a seed in the starter kit will usually germinate in the first 7-14 days. I've had parsley take as long as four weeks and I've had basil germinate in 48 hours.

When a seedling first emerges it craves light and since some seeds actually require light to germinate, I will turn on the grow lights or place the kit in a window box immediately after planting. It's a low feeling to come home from work and find that a little basil sprouted only to fall over and die from a lack of light.

Seedling Pots

There are a lot of different options available when it comes to selecting the pot you want to grow your seedlings in. In a pinch I've even used a 22 ounce red drink cup with a couple of pin holes in the bottom!

The tender roots of herbs can be subject to transplant shock when removed from their seedling pot. A plastic seedling pot is a cheap option but it increases the chances of transplant shock during its first week in the garden. For some herbs like oregano and rosemary transplant shock is nearly a nonfactor. For more tender herbs like Basil, transplant shock out of a plastic seed pot is a very strong possibility.

The ideal seed pot is one that biodegrades shortly after planting in the garden. There are several options available to you in the form of peat pots. These pots are made from dried and compressed peat moss. When planted in the moist soil of the garden they begin to break up and allow the plant's roots to grow through them within a week or so.

For the do-it-yourselfer there is the option of making your own pots from newspaper. The Newspaper option will indeed save you money but it will also cost you time and hassle. The basic premise is to find an object like a large tomato can or a wine bottle and wrap multiple layers of newspaper around it. Then secure the seams with paper tape or organic white glue.

Paper mache is also an option for shaping and securing a pot made from newspaper and can be a fun way to dragoon your children into helping you. They get to feel like they are a part of the process and take part in watching their little plant grow. You get nimble little fingers that help save you time.

If you choose to make your own seedling pots from newspaper you will want to make sure the newspaper you source is printed with soy based inks and the tape or glue you use is biodegradable. Most non-glossy newsprint these days is made with inexpensive soy based inks but a quick call to the newspaper will confirm it for you.

Having worked with homemade newspaper pots in the past, they are not the ideal for herbs that will spend more than two to three weeks indoors. After successive watering the newspaper tends to break down and weaken. It often splits at the seam or in the middle of the pot.

Since most herbs require six to ten weeks indoors, you will ultimately have to put a newspaper based pot inside of a plastic container in order to make up for the structural weakness. Or take the paper mache option.

Size

When it comes to selecting the size of seed pot you want to use, bigger is almost always better. Herbs need a lot of water to feed tender, aromatic foliage. This means their roots like to spread. As a good rule of thumb, I wouldn't advise going smaller than a 4 inch diameter seed pot for any herb. If you've got the space, a six inch diameter pot would be even better!

Soil

While the peat moss of the soil plugs is the ideal medium of germinating plants and giving young tender roots something to grab a hold of, it is still low in nutrients. A sterile potting mix is preferable to using garden soil. Garden soil can hide fungus spores and pests that a young seedling lacks the strength to resist.

It is possible to mix garden soil with vermiculite and a little sand and sterilize it in small batches in a 180 degree oven. You don't want to heat it over 180 degrees because it might damage the chemical structure of key soil nutrients. Test the temperature of the soil by inserting a meat probe into the middle of the batch. I can also tell you from experience that you should not expect a smile on their face when your spouse comes home to a house that stinks of burning dirt!

Choosing the Herbs

In early January seed catalogs begin flooding mailboxes as a world of opportunities and ideas explodes into a gardener's imagination. It's easy to thumb through pages and pages of lush green photography full of gardening articles and end up with a too-long laundry list of things you want to grow.

I have to admit that more than once I have gotten myself in over my head by trying to grow too many plants in a greenhouse too small for all my great ideas. Before you start planning out a hedge maze of rosemary or making plans to line your driveway with basil you will really want to make a plan that defines your limits and stick to it. A crowded garden is an unproductive garden and a stressed out gardener is missing out on the therapeutic relaxation that comes from putting your hands in the soil.

I start out every year making a garden plan. I draw out my garden in scale on graph paper and sketch up my ideas before I even order the first packet of seeds. Coming up with a couple of rough drafts is a good way to get an idea of the number of plants you can grow without getting in over your head.

Another thing to consider is growing herbs in containers. A five gallon bucket full of potting soil inside of a wood shell with herbs growing out of it can be as visually attractive on your patio as it is practical for your kitchen.

Planting and preparing your plants for life outside

Young seedlings that have only known the windless warm world of life indoors can rarely handle direct transplanting into the garden soil. Instead they usually require a two week period of hardening. Starting two weeks before your planned planting day you will want to put the plants outside each morning before you go to work and bring them inside each night before sundown.

If there is inclement weather or it is going to be unseasonably cold that day it is best to skip that day of hardening and leave the seedlings indoors. If you leave for work early and the temperature outside is 34 degrees or below, you should skip that day of hardening. Another rule of thumb to follow is that seedlings should not be outside on a day when the forecasted high is 39 degrees or below. The physical properties of water begin to change at that temperature and this has the effect of poor nutrient up take in the plants roots.

Preparation is your best friend when it comes to preparing for planting day. Even though you might have waited for the average last frost date for your region, there is still a chance of a freak frost. Make sure you check the advanced forecast for any potential frost. Any time you see the overnight low forecasted for 36 degrees or colder you should plan on covering the plants.

Tilling the garden is about more than just making the ground soft enough for you to get a shovel into, it's also about providing soft soil for young roots to expand into as well as providing aeration. If you don't own a tiller and can't rent one, you can always use a spade shovel to spot till planting areas. When you spot till and area you want to loosen the soil in an area at least 2 feet in diameter and at least 18 inches deep per each plant.

When you planting the seedling remember that the soil needs to be kept loose. Only a very light amount of hand tamping near the base of the plant is required to help seat it in the hole. If you are concerned about the wind blowing it over you can drive a small wooden stake into the soil and lightly tie the plants stem to it using cotton twine. Water the plant thoroughly once it is planted, preferably with warm water.

If you suffer the misfortune of having planted all of your herbs and a freak frost warning you will have to cover the herbs the night before. Remember the coldest time will be the hours just before dawn. Let the plant capture the warm part of the sun the day before and then cover a few hours before sunset.

Watering the plant especially with warm water will help protect the roots and allow the soil to help retain some heat energy overnight. When covering the plants an old sheet is a better insulator than a plastic tarp. Covering the plant with a 5 gallon bucket is also an option. Once in a moment of desperation when I planted more than I had sheets and buckets for I did very well burying the plants inside mounds of fluffy straw. However this made for a lot of work delicately removing the straw the next day.

Do not uncover the plants again until the all threat of frost as passed. If there are back to back frost events in the forecast you can leave them plants covered for a full day and they will survive.

Each type of herb has its own unique needs through the course of a growing season. In the next section I will break each herb down to help you better understand how to grow it in the garden and cook with it in the kitchen.

Chapter 3 – Beloved Basil

Growing Basil

Basil is most commonly known as one of the essential herbs in Italian cuisine. It has a history that traces itself back into antiquity. Originally speculated to have originated in India, it has spread across multiple continents. Basil comes in many different varieties that have found a place in several ethnic cuisines. However most of what you find in America these days is forms of mammoth or sweet Genovese basil.

Basil grows a large bushy plant with large jade colored leaves. It prefers to grow in full sun when well watered. However since the upper leaves can sometimes suffer from sun scald you will get a larger total yield if you plant it in a location that has light shade in the afternoon.

Basil does poorly if you attempt to bring it indoors for the winter as the upper leaves tend to shade out the lower leaves and the new growth emerging from the stem. However if you grew the basil in a container during the summer you can often extend the season by bringing it indoors and placing it in a sunny window. Rotating the planter 90 degrees each day and water it with warm water can buy you as much as four to six weeks of life.

Cooking with Basil

Basil is often one of the most expensive herbs in the grocery store is wilted. Even then what's offered is usually some half dead weak version of the vibrant aromatic magic you can pick fresh from your own garden.

Incorporating basil into a cooked sauce accents its flavor, while using it fresh or whole in meat dishes accents its aromatics. Basil also can play a vibrant role many salads and has even made forays into the world of desserts.

A chiffonade is a common way to chop basil. Simply stack the leaves from largest to smallest. Roll them up like a miniature cigar. Then using a chef's knife cut the roll into 1/8th inch sections. When the roll releases you will have many small ribbons of basil. These ribbons of basil are a great way to garnish a dish.

Basil featured recipes

Pesto

Pesto is the quintessential application of Basil. This classic Italian sauce is easy to make and goes great as tossed with pasta or served alongside meat. Pesto pairs well with beef, chicken, lamb and shrimp.

A pesto sauce is traditionally made with basil, garlic, olive oil, parmesan cheese and pine nuts. Pine nuts can sometimes be expensive. It can often feel ridiculous to go through the effort of growing your own basil to cut cost, only to spend fifty dollars in pine nuts over the course of the summer. Pistachio nuts are an inexpensive substitution, which allows you to bring the price down without sacrificing texture or quality.

Yes if an Italian purist was in the kitchen and saw you using pistachio nuts they would probably back hand you. To be honest I think the difference is minimal. Just be mindful to choose unsalted pistachios. If the only pistachio nuts you can find are salted, then reduce the salt in the recipe below by half.

Equipment

Food Processor

Work Bowl

Ingredients

4 Tablespoons pistachio or pine nuts

2 Garlic cloves, peeled

3 Tablespoons extra-virgin olive oil

4 Cups basil leaves

1/2 Cup fresh Parmesan cheese, grated

1/4 teaspoon salt

Procedure

Step 1: Run the motor of your food processor as you drop the pine (or pistachio) nuts and garlic through the feeder chute. Process until minced.

Step 2: Drizzle the olive oil slowly and pulse three times.

Step 3: Add the basil, Parmesan cheese and salt. Pulse 3 to 5 times until you have a smooth green sauce.

When pairing pasta with pesto sauce the texture of the pasta often dictates how the two should be combined. I find that with a smooth noodle such as linguini or fettuccini that it is best to serve the dish pesto on top or on the side. This is especially true if the dish is served with a whole meat such as shrimp or a fillet of chicken. Along with the visual appeal, allowing the sauce on the side gives the diner the option of dipping the meat in it or tossing the pesto into the pasta.

If a textured noodle is used or a meat is integrated into the dish, then I prefer to toss the pasta with the pesto. The main reason for this is to allow the pesto sauce to impregnate all the textures and contours of the pasta.

Pesto is best if lightly warmed and then added to the dish. The natural oils and flavor compounds that give basil its aromatic qualities are fleeting when exposed to heat. Thus a short cooking time is preferred.

Frittatas

Frittatas are most commonly used as a breakfast dish or casserole. The modern day “Breakfast Bake” casserole essentially evolved out of a classic frittata recipe. What has now become a mishmash of bacon eggs and vegetables tossed with toasted corn cereal, started life as a delicate and herbaceous meal. The 20th century was not kind to the frittata. With the renewed interest in scratch made cooking and whole foods, this dish is finding a renaissance at breakfast as well as the supper table.

Equipment

10 inch cast iron skillet or oven safe pan

Non-stick frying pan

Work Bowl

Whisk

Ingredients

6 Whole large eggs

4 Egg whites

2 Ounces parmesan cheese, shredded

1/2 Teaspoon fresh cracked black pepper

1/2 Cup basil leaves, chiffonade

1 Tablespoon of fresh oregano, chopped

3 Tablespoons olive oil

1/2 A large red onion, julienned

2 Cloves of garlic, minced

6 Slices bacon or cured ham, chopped

2 Cups sliced mushrooms, cleaned and sliced

8 Ounces of asparagus or 1/3rd of a green bell pepper trimmed to 1 inch pieces

Procedure

Step 1: Preheat your oven to 400 degrees.

Step 2: In a large work bowl whisk together the eggs, egg whites, Parmesan cheese and black pepper. You can reserve the mixture in your refrigerator for up to one hour.

Step 3: In a 10 inch cast iron skillet or oven safe pan, heat 2 tablespoons of olive oil over medium-low heat. Add all of the vegetables except the garlic and sweat them until the onion begins to take a little color. Approximately 5 to 7 minutes.

Step 4: Once your vegetables have started sweating add your bacon or chopped ham to a separate non-stick pan. Cook the meat thoroughly, approximately 5 to 7 minutes.

Step 5: Add one tablespoon of olive oil to the 10 inch skillet and combine meat and vegetables. Add the minced garlic. Pour the egg mixture into the pan and tilt to evenly distribute.

Step 6: Sprinkle the herbs lightly over top jiggle the pan to help them incorporate. Then sprinkle on the cheese. Place the pan in the oven and bake until top is lightly browned and eggs are fully set.

Cook time approximately 10 to 12 minutes.

Step 7: Once the eggs have set and the top is browned remove the pan from oven and let it cool slightly.

Cut into 6 pie shaped wedges.

Serving with a side of a tomato and parsley chutney and/or a dollop of seasoned sour cream is a nice touch as the cool component will play well against the heat and richness of the frittata.

Basil Sorbet

This is a sweet savory dish that can be used a palette cleanser or as a desert course. The coolness and sweetness of the sorbet plays well with the aromatic elements of basil. Adding lemon juice can take the sorbet towards the sweet desert end of the flavor spectrum. While adding a few table spoons of pureed cherry tomatoes can highlight basil's savory aspect.

Equipment

An ice cream/sorbet maker

A large work bowl with a cover

Silicone Spatula

Ingredients

2 Cups water

2 Cups granulated white sugar

1 Tablespoon lemon zest (Sweet) or 3 Tablespoons pureed cherry tomato (Savory)

2 Cups fresh basil (rough chopped and packed)

1/8th Teaspoon salt

1 Cup fresh lemon juice

Procedure

Step 1: Make a simple syrup by simmering the water on low heat before adding, sugar and lemon zest. Cook mixture until the sugar is fully dissolved. Remove from heat.

Step 2: Add the basil and salt. Let the mixture steep and cool down for half an hour at room temperature before stirring in the lemon juice.

You can cover and refrigerate overnight.

Step 3: Two hours before you plan to serve, strain the mix through a fine mesh sieve.

Step 4: Turn on the ice cream maker and slowly pour the mixture into the core. (Or otherwise follow manufacturer's instruction).

Step 5: Allow the mixture to run until it thickens to the consistency of soft serve ice cream. Approximately 20 minutes. If you are making a savory sorbet, you can add the chopped cherry tomatoes at any time once the ice cream maker is in motion.

Step 6: Scrape the sorbet from the core into a large work bowl. Lid and place in the freezer for one and a half to two hours to harden.

The Sorbet is best served in a parfait glass with a garnish of basil cut in chiffonade ribbons.

Basil is an herb that works and plays well in so many applications that it is only limited by your imagination. If you love basil and you don't want to drain your bank account buying wilted leaves at the grocery store, then it's well worth the time to learn how to grow your own!

Chapter 4 – Cherish the Chives

Growing Chives

Chives are a perennial herb available in classic onion and garlic varieties. They are members of the allium family along with onions and garlic. As such they prefer cool soil temperatures and afternoon shade.

Chives are easily grown from seed. Their first year they are not yet frost hardy, so if you do grow them from seed plan to start them indoors 10 weeks before the average frost date. After the first year this frost hardy perennial will be able to survive all winter long with little more than an insulating layer of mulch or straw.

However if you plant chives in a one or two gallon container you can then bring them in during the winter and they will do quite well in a window box if you rotate the planter 180 degrees every two days.

Chives should be harvested before individual strands make seed heads. When harvesting cut near the soil line. Be mindful not to cut any of the white bulb root core.

Cooking with chives

Chives have a mild onion flavor that is also pervasive and long lasting. Chives are a great way to add the aromatic flavor or onion to a dish without having it dominate a diner's palette. Since they are a vibrant green they also add visual appeal as a topping or a garnish to many dishes.

Chive featured recipes

Garlic Chive Mashed Potatoes

Cream cheese, milk, and chives add richness and flavor to mashed potatoes. While this recipes calls for russet potatoes unpeeled red potatoes are also a nice substitution for added color and nutrition.

Equipment

A large cook pot

Colander

Potato Ricer

Silicone Spatula

Ingredients

10 Medium russet potatoes, peeled and cut in half

4 Ounce cream cheese, cut into cubes

4 Tablespoons of butter

4 Cloves of garlic, whole and peeled

3/4 Cup hot milk

1-1/4 Teaspoons salt

1/2 Teaspoon fresh cracked black pepper

1/2 Cup chopped fresh garlic chives

Procedure

Step 1: Add the cloves of garlic to the pot with the potatoes. Cover with 2 inches of water and boil gently until potatoes are tender. Cook time approximately 15 minutes.

Step 2: Drain and return to the pan with the heat off. Pass potato halves and garlic cloves through the potato ricer for a fine texture. If you are using red potatoes a rough mash with a potato masher is better.

Step 3: Add the butter, cream cheese, milk, salt and pepper. Fold them together with the silicone spatula.

Step 4: Once combined fold in the garlic chives and prepare for service.

By adding the chives at the end it refreshes the aromatic component of garlic. The garlic flavor of the chives lends itself best to red meat dishes. These flavor profiles pair well with a medium red wine like a Pinot Noir or Shiraz.

Sour cream and onion dip

For decades the classic form of this dip was to stir processed French onion soup mix with sour cream. Wait one hour for the flavors to meld and your party goers could double dip their chips with reckless abandon into a sea of salt, onion powder and rich sour cream.

If you are looking for an alternative to this dip that uses fresh ingredients instead of twenty-six letter long preservatives, then chives can bring flavor as well as visual appeal. This is also a great topping for baked potatoes, potato gratin or used as a condiment alongside a frittata or omelet.

Equipment

A medium work bowl with a lid

A mixing spoon

Serving tray or bowl for holding dip

Ingredients *Multiply ingredients to match the number of diners as needed.*

1 Cup of sour cream (Fat content your preference)

1 Tablespoon cold milk

1 Tablespoon fresh lemon juice

1/2 Cup chopped chives

1/2 Teaspoon of smoked paprika or old bay

1/2 Cup of red onion (Minced)

Pinch of Salt

1/4 Teaspoon fresh cracked black pepper

Procedure

Prepare this dip two hours before you plan to serve. The additional time sitting in the refrigerator will allow the flavors to meld.

Step 1: Place sour cream, milk and lemon juice in the work bowl and stir aggressively until the mixture is smooth.

Step 2: Fold in chopped chives, smoked paprika, salt and pepper.

Step 3: Cover and refrigerate for up to two hours.

This recipe serves 2-4 guests depending on what other snacks and side dishes you offer. For a natural flavored dip like this I recommend plain or kettle cooked potato chips to other flavored and over seasoned varieties. The artificial flavorings can drown out the subtle earthy notes of the chives.

Chapter 5 – Save room for Cilantro

Cilantro is an herb used primarily in Chinese, Indian and Mexican Cuisine.

It is best to start from seed and make staggered successive plantings through the season. Cilantro struggles to germinate some times in warm soil so it is best to start it in small peat pots without using the heated potting tray. Cilantro does well when planted in containers, however high heat causes it to bolt to seed. Polyurethane foam or wooden planters are a good choice for container growing cilantro as they help insulate the soil.

Cilantro should be planted in a location that gets good morning sun and moderate shade in the afternoon. Keep the soil covered and well watered. Every time you harvest a cilantro you should plant more seeds in its place to maintain fresh successive plantings through the season.

The seeds of cilantro can be harvested and ground into the spice coriander.

Cooking with Cilantro

Fresh cilantro has an intense fresh flavor. If you are too heavy handed with cilantro it can quickly take over a dish. Cilantro and coriander both have medicinal qualities as a diaphoretic as well as an appetite stimulant.

Cilantro feature recipes

Pico de Gallo

This is the quintessential condiment used in many forms of authentic Mexican cooking. You can use it to dress tacos, fajitas, spoon over a soup, serve alongside an entrée or simply use as a dip for chips. Pico de Gallo is a condiment that brings freshness and life to just about any dish.

Equipment

Small Work Bowl

Silicone Spatula

Lime juicer or press

Ingredients

2 Plum tomatoes (or 1 cup of cherry tomatoes) diced

1 Medium red onion, chopped fine

1 Jalapeno pepper, seeded and chopped

2 Sprigs fresh cilantro, chopped fine

1 Clove of garlic chopped fine

1/8 Teaspoon sea salt

1/8 Teaspoon fresh cracked black pepper

The juice of 1 lime

Procedure

Step 1: Wash and chop all vegetables and place in a medium work bowl.

Step 2: Add salt and pepper

Step 3: Pour the lime juice over the top folding with a silicone spatula to integrate all ingredients.

Step 4: Refrigerate for a half hour before service to allow the flavors to meld and the Pico de Gallo to chill.

Step 5: Taste to check the strength of the Cilantro. If you want more herb flavor, chop and sprinkle more and toss lightly.

Salsa Verde

This fresh salsa is made from tomatillos (Green husk tomatoes), cilantro, garlic and peppers. You can serve it as a condiment, make it into a soup or can it as a salsa.

Equipment

Hot pan or a cast iron griddle

Food processor

Large work bowl

Large cook pot

Ingredients

1 Pound tomatillos, husked and washed

1 Medium yellow onion, chopped

4 Cloves garlic, pan roasted

4 Tablespoons cilantro, rough chopped

2 Jalapeno peppers, seeded and chopped fine

1/4 Teaspoon ground cumin

1/8 Teaspoon sugar

Salt and fresh cracked black pepper

Procedure

Step 1: Remove and discard husks from tomatillos and wash the natural stickiness with warm water. While you are cleaning the Tomatillos, heat a hot pan or skillet on the range or grill.

Step 2: Place the garlic peppers and tomatillos in the hot pan and dry roast them to activate the sugars. This heating brings out the depth of flavor. Stir constantly until you see the garlic turn dark brown or the skins of the tomatillos get black spots.

Step 3: Remove the ingredients to a large work bowl and allow them to cool down for 15 to 20 minutes.

Step 4: Add all ingredients into the food processor. Make sure to include any liquid from the work bowl. Pulse the food processor until the ingredients take on the consistency of a chunky salsa.

Salsa Verde can be served chilled as a dip for chips or a cool condiment for tacos and fajitas. It can be canned and will keep up to two years. It can also be used in cooked applications such as white chili.

Chapter 6 – Don't forget about Dill

When most of us think of dill we immediately think of it as the essential herb for canning pickles. However dill has a long and storied history through many cuisines across Europe, Asia and parts of the Middle East. In fact Dill is a very most popular herb in Scandinavian cooking.

Dill is usually available in many garden nurseries but is also easily grown from seed. Since dill grows quickly and can bolt to seed in warm soil temps. You don't need to start seeds indoors any sooner than two weeks before the average last frost date for your area.

Dill seed and the fronds/leaves both have culinary uses. Deciding which you prefer is an important aspect of selecting the growing site. In warm soil temps dill bolts to seed, so for someone who is interested in dill seed, a full sun location would be better.

More commonly people grow dill for the use of the fronds or foliage. In order to keep the plants from prematurely bolting to seed you should select a location with good eastern light in the morning and light to dappled shade in the afternoon.

Dill is also rather delicate and high wind exposure can damage fronds and stems. It also should not be planted near cilantro or fennel as they are in the same family and cross pollination can cause issues in flavor profiles and seed saving.

Dill does not like drying out, so make sure to keep it well watered. A light layer of straw mulch can help a lot during a heat wave.

Cooking with Dill

Dill brings zesty yet earthy flavor to dishes it is seasoned with. The same flavor profile that traditionally lights up pickled cucumbers also brings brightness and depth to seafood dishes.

Dill featured recipes

Dill Marinated Whitefish with cucumber chutney

It's quite possible that Great Lakes Whitefish is one of the most underappreciated fish in America. It can be a little bony and needs a slow cooking application in order to help the clean white meat pull easily from the bone.

The Whitefish is marinated in dill and garlic vinegar before being baked. It can be eaten hot or allowed to cool in the refrigerator for up to two days before being dressed with a refreshing dill and cucumber chutney. The chilled application is a great meal or snack for hot summer days.

Equipment

Zip top bag (Gallon size)

Baking rack or half sheet pan

Medium size work bowl with lid

Gallon size zip top bag

Ingredients

Whitefish preparation

Vegetable oil

2 Fillets of white fish (approximately 4 pounds) Trimmed of any fatty edges.

2 Cups coarsely chopped fresh dill

1 Medium red onion (chopped)

1 Teaspoon coarse ground sea salt

1/4 Teaspoon ground pepper

6 Tablespoons rice wine vinegar

Chutney

4 cups cucumber, diced peeled seeded

1 Cup cherry tomatoes (chopped)

1/2 cup chopped fresh dill

1/4 cup rice wine vinegar

4 teaspoons coarse ground sea salt

Procedure

Prepare and marinated the fish the night before you plan to cook.

Step 1: Finely chop dill and onion. Sprinkle each fillet with salt and pepper. Gently massage the dill and onion mixture into the fish. Carefully slide the fillets into a gallon size zip top bag before slowly pouring the vinegar over them. Seal the bag and chill overnight.

Step 2: The next day preheat your oven to 350 degrees. Move the fish from the bag to an oven rack. Bake uncovered for 25 to 30 minutes.

Step 3: Serve hot or let stand at room temperature 30 minutes. You can cover and chill at least 2 hours in the refrigerator as this dish is also delicious and refreshing when served chilled.

Chutney recipe

Step 1: In medium bowl combine diced cherry tomatoes with cucumber, dill, vinegar and salt.

Step 2: Let stand in refrigerator for 2 hours. Stir occasionally. Season the chutney with fresh cracked black pepper right before service.

For service: Remove any loose dill from fillets. Cut crosswise into portions. Slide spatula or large metal spoon under each, separating the meat from the skin.

Arrange fish on plates. Drain any excess water from the chutney and spoon over fillets. Dress the remaining chutney on the side.

Pickled Asparagus

The process for pickling asparagus is very similar to pickling cucumbers. Pickled Asparagus is an application that exists just as much out of a sense of practicality as it does flavor. Dill tends to either bolt or bush out faster than you can use it around the same point in summer that mature asparagus can start to get woody. So this is a great way to make the most out of both bounties.

Equipment

5 pint jars, washed and sterilized

Large cook pot

Canning pot or stock pot

Washed rings

New canning lids

Ingredients

5 Pounds fresh asparagus, washed, cleaned and cut into 4 inch spears

2 Cups rice wine vinegar

2-1/2 Cups water

2 Teaspoons mustard seed

1 Tablespoon pickling spice, in a spice bag or tea ball

2 Tablespoons pickling salt

1 Teaspoon granulated sugar

In each jar add

Dash cayenne pepper

1 teaspoon fresh dill, chopped

1 whole clove garlic

Procedure

Step 1: Place trimmed and washed asparagus spears in boiling water. Blanch for two minutes. Place garlic, dill and cayenne pepper in bottom of each jar. Pack the asparagus spears into each jar in an upright position.

Step 2: Combine vinegar, water, pickling salt, mustard seed, sugar and tea ball of pickling spice into saucepan and boil. Turn off the heat and steep for 10 minutes. Remove the tea ball and discard.

Step 3: Pour brine over asparagus and seal the jars with rings and new lids.

Step 4: Place jars into canner of boiling water for 10 minutes. Cool.

Store the jars in a cool, dark place. Pickled asparagus is a nice element for a snack tray. It pairs well with pickled fish, smoky cheese and a white wine like Pinot Grigio.

Creamy Mustard and Dill Sauce

This sauce is a great accompaniment for any white meat dish. You can add a fine chopped dill pickle to this recipe if you want a new take on tartar sauce. The sauce can be made 24 hours in advance and refrigerated. The additional time will help the flavors to meld.

Equipment

Medium work bowl with lid

Silicone spatula

Ingredients

1 Tablespoon dry mustard powder

2 Tablespoons fresh lemon juice

1 Cup mayonnaise

1/3 Cup sour cream

1/4 Cup stone ground mustard

3 Tablespoons fresh dill chopped

1 Tablespoon smoked paprika or old bay

Coarse ground sea salt and fresh cracked black pepper

Procedure

Step 1: Combine dry mustard powder and lemon juice in a medium work bowl. Wait 2-3 minutes for the lemon juice to hydrate the mustard powder.

Step 2: Add the mayonnaise, sour cream, stone ground mustard and dill. Fold together with a silicone spatula until properly combined.

Step 3: Stir in smoked paprika and old bay. Taste and add salt, pepper or more lemon juice if desired.

This sauce can be covered and refrigerated for up to a day.

Chapter 7 – Be mindful of Mint

Mint is an herb that is best grown in a container. Mint propagates itself by sending out root runners as well as self-seeding. If you plant it uncontained in a garden it will slowly begin to take over and crowd out other plants. If you don't want to container plant mint you should still cut the bottom off of a 5 gallon bucket and sink it into the soil. The root runners cannot exceed a depth of 12-14 inches.

If you intend to save your own heirloom mint seeds it is important to note that Mint is a promiscuous pollinator and as a result tends not to breed true. If mint is allowed to cross pollinate the resulting new seed will usually create a plant with a muted mint flavor. If you want to grow two different types of mint you will want to separate them in pollination isolation by a distance of at least 400 feet.

There are literally hundreds of different varieties of mint. In fact the mint family even includes catnip. However the two most popular varieties of mint are peppermint and spearmint. For my personal tastes I find peppermint to be the more multipurpose of the two.

While you can find mint seeds from reputable vendors it is probably easier to simply buy the plants you want from a nursery store in late spring. When it comes to determining the number of plants you want to buy I recommend three. Through the course of a growing season you should be able to harvest enough mint to keep the family in julep, jelly and mint ice cream by rotating your harvest through three plants. At the end of the season you can then completely harvest all three plants and dry them for tea.

Growing Mint

While mint seeds prefer to germinate in soil around 70 degrees, the ideal growing conditions through the main season calls for partial shade. Mint is a natural deterrent for several insects that plague cucumbers. Mint planted in a container behind a trellis of cucumber vines is an excellent companion planting option for both plants as well as a great way to save space in the garden!

Through the season mint prefers cool soil temps and modestly watered soil. Sandy soil should be avoided. Garden soil or rich loam is preferred for their water retention qualities. Early in the season mint will enjoy a helping hand from a weekly dosage of a nitrogen rich fertilizer. After a month the plant should be established and will require no additional fertilizer through the season.

Mint leaves can be harvested at any point after the plant has established itself. However you should try to never harvest more than half of a plant's leaves at a time.

Mint planted in a container or planter does poorly if you attempt to over winter it indoors. When placed under grow lights or in a sunny window the upper leaves tend to shade the lower leaves. The best you can hope for is extending the season by placing the planter in a sunny window with a southern exposure and rotating the planter 90 degrees daily.

If you live in Growing Zone 5 or warmer mint will survive in a planter outdoors over the winter if you bury the planter in the ground and cover it with 4-6 inches of straw.

Mint Featured Recipes

Mint Ice Cream

One of my favorite summer time treats is mint chocolate chip ice cream made with fresh mint straight from the garden. Commercially produced mint ice cream is made from distilled extracts, which tend to pull only one flavor note out of the mint oils. Fresh mint from the garden, steeped in cream creates an entire symphony of earthy yet minty flavors that melt on your tongue while cooling and cleansing your palette.

If you are used to mint ice cream being a radioactive shade of green, you will want to add some green food coloring. Fresh Mint will only produce a pale green ice cream.

Equipment

Ice Cream Maker

Medium Sauce Pot

A large work bowl

2 Tea Balls

Ingredients

2 Cups Milk

2 Cups Heavy Cream

1 Cup Sugar

1/2 Teaspoon Salt

1 Tablespoon Vanilla

8 Tablespoons Peppermint, bruised and rough chopped

(Optional) Green Food Coloring

(Optional) 3 Tablespoons semi-sweet chocolate chips, chopped

Procedure

Step 1: Pour the heavy cream into a small sauce pot on low heat.

Step 2: Bruise the mint leaves gently with your thumb and forefinger before rough chopping them. This will maximize the mint oils released. Turn off the heat and place the tea balls into the tea balls and set them in the heavy cream. Steep the mint for 20 minutes.

Step 3: Remove the tea balls and stir in the sugar. Once the sugar is dissolved place the pot in the freezer to chill for approximately a half hour, check periodically and scrape any ice crystals that might form on the side of the pot.

Step 4: Add all ingredients together in a large work bowl and stir thoroughly to combine. If you prefer to have chocolate pieces in your ice cream this is the stage to add them in.

Step 5: Follow the manufacturer's instructions for your ice cream maker.

Step 6: In general, after a half hour in the ice cream maker the mixture will have the consistency of soft serve ice cream. Scrape the mixture back into the large work bowl and place it in the freezer for 1-2 hours until it hardens to your desired level of firmness.

Peppermint or Spearmint Tea

You will inevitably come to a point in early Fall when a hard frost is eminent in the forecast and you'll be forced to harvest all of the mint. This is a great time to dry mint leaves to be stored for tea. Mint tea has many great health properties. It is a spasmolytic muscle relaxer. Its carminative properties help with gas and indigestion. Mint tea is also a natural expectorant which is great for winter head and chest colds.

Harvest the leaves careful to avoid getting stems into the batch. Wash and pat them dry on a paper towel. Some cats will actually respond to dry mint stems the same way they do catnip, so don't ignore the stems value as a pet treat.

When drying mint it is best to array the leaves in single layer on the top trays of a food dehydrator. However if you don't have a food dehydrator you can get by in a pinch by placing the mint on a draining rack set on a sheet pan in a 180 degree oven.

Regardless of the drying application you choose, the leaves will be completely dried when you can crush them between thumb and forefinger.

The ideal storage is to use a sealable air tight glass jar.

Chapter 8 – The olfactory magic of Oregano

Oregano is a low lying bushy herb that grows its leaves on tendril like stems. It is a staple in Italian cooking with many uses in Mediterranean cuisine. In my opinion Greek Oregano is the more aromatic and flavorful choice compared to the common o. vulgare.

Oregano is easy to start from seed. It enjoys warm soil and sunny conditions. If you plan on container growing oregano you will want to plant it alone or with its tall standing cousin marjoram. Since it seeds itself over the course of a growing season it will eventually take over any container you plant it in.

Since oregano reseeds itself you will need to pot it up to a larger pot every year to keep it from getting root bound.

You can easily bring container grown oregano indoors. It does well growing under grow lights or in a window box, so long as you water it with warm water. A purple coloration under the leaves is a sign of low phosphorus. This tends to be an issue when oregano is placed under grow lights more than sunlight. The leaves are fine to eat, simply fertilize the plant with a phosphorus rich fertilizer.

Cooking with oregano

An Italian Chef once told me that if you can't think of a dish that could use oregano you're simply not trying. It goes perfectly with meat, cheese, vegetables, soups and stews. The primary limitation of oregano is your imagination.

Oregano also has medicinal properties as a carminative that helps prevent gas. Its anti-spasmodic qualities help with muscle spasms, cramps and aches.

Oregano featured recipes

Oregano infused olive oil

This olive oil is a great addition to the pantry for sautéing vegetables or using as the oil base in a vinaigrette salad dressing. Be mindful that you will want to allow the oil to infuse for a minimum of two weeks before using.

Equipment

Oil glass bottle

Funnel

A glass bowl with a lid or plastic wrap

Ingredients

1/2 cup of fresh picked, washed oregano

4 cups of extra-virgin olive oil

Procedure

Step 1: Wash the oregano and pat dry with a paper towel. Allow 10 minutes for any residual moisture to dry.

Step 2: Lightly bruise the leaves with your finger tips to help release flavor. Place them in a clean glass container, cover with warmed oil, and seal tightly. Leave in a cool, dark place for at least two weeks.

Step 3: If after two weeks you feel the flavor is not strong enough for your taste you can add more fresh herbs and let stand another week.

Step 4: Pour the oil into a decorate glass bottle with a pour spout. You can strain the herbs out of oil with a fine mesh sieve. You can leave the herbs in the oil but be mindful that the flavor will become stronger over time.

Homemade Pizza Sauce

Since oregano is considered the quintessential pizza sauce herb. I would be remiss if I didn't offer at least one recipe for a pizza sauce you can make at home.

Equipment

Medium sauce pot

Ladle

Ingredients

1 Can diced tomatoes

1 Small yellow onion, chopped fine

2 Cloves of garlic, minced

4 Leaves of fresh basil, chopped

1 Tablespoon fresh oregano, Chopped

Pinch salt

Pinch fresh ground black pepper

Pinch sugar

2 tablespoons olive oil or oregano infused olive oil

Procedure

Step 1: Add olive oil to a medium sauce pot over a medium high heat. Allow a few minutes for the oil to come up to temp.

Step 2: Add the onions and sauté until they start becoming translucent. Add the garlic and sauté for one minute until golden.

Step 3: Add the can of crushed tomato. Stir well and bring to a simmer.

Step 4: Add the basil, oregano, salt and pepper. Simmer on a low heat, stirring occasionally for 15 minutes.

Step 5: Taste the sauce, if it seems a bit green or bitter, add a pinch of sugar.

This sauce is best if used immediately when dressing the pizza. However it is also an excellent dip for garlic bread or cheese sticks.

Chapter 9 – Parsley is the perfect partner

Parsley is a great herb for adding color and aromatic flavor to many dishes, since it grows well indoors under grow lights it is a strong candidate for container planting.

When growing Parsley from seed it can take a long time to germinate if not given proper bottom heat. If you aren't using a heated potting tray you will want to start parsley 10-12 weeks before the average last frost date for your region. If you do use a heated potting tray you can start parsley 6 weeks before the average last frost date.

While you can find parley in garden supply stores each spring the cost is much higher than growing from seed. In general it takes two weeks for a well picked parsley plant to regenerate itself during peak season. I personally rotate through 8 plants each season, then bring the four indoors over the winter. This makes growing from seed to be far more cost effective.

Parsley forms a shallow sprawling root ball so you are growing it in a container you will want to look for a planter that gives it room to grow and spread. A shallow root ball means you will want to mulch the top of the planter or accept that you will need to water it frequently.

Parsley grows well if brought indoors in the winter and placed under grow lights or in a sunny window.

Cooking with parsley

Parsley is very aromatic as a result it loses some of its magic when cooked in high heat applications. When added to soups and broths that also call for aromatic vegetables it helps accent the flavors. Parsleys aromatic nature also helps enhance the flavor of acidic fruits and sauces.

Parsley is a nice substitution for people who find the taste of cilantro to be too strong.

Parley featured recipes

Parsley and tomato chutney

This tomato chutney is an excellent side for heavy dishes. It really shines alongside an omelet or frittata.

Ingredients

1 Cup of cherry tomatoes

1 Tablespoon red onion, minced

1/4 Cup parsley, chopped fine

1 Tablespoon fresh lemon juice

1/2 Teaspoon fresh cracked black pepper

A pinch of coarse ground sea salt or kosher salt

Procedure

Step 1: Chop the cherry tomatoes by cutting them in half lengthwise and remove any seeds that come out easily. Then chop the halves into quarters.

Step 2: Chop and combine onion and parsley. Add to the tomatoes.

Step 3: Squeeze the lemon juice and toss all ingredients to combine.

Chimichurri Sauce

This sauce traces its origins to the meat centric cuisine of Argentina. While it is the perfect accompaniment to a grilled steak, it can also shine as a condiment for sausage or added to lettuce wraps and spring rolls.

The aromatic power of the parsley really lifts the earthy heat of the garlic and onions. The spicy notes of a quality olive oil will also be enhanced by parsley.

Equipment

Food Processor

Ingredients

1 Cup fresh parsley, packed

6 Cloves garlic, minced

1/2 Cup extra virgin olive oil

1/4 Cup rice wine vinegar

Juice from half lemon

1/2 Small red onion, minced

1 Tablespoon fresh oregano

1 Teaspoon fresh cracked black pepper

1/2 Teaspoon salt

Procedure

Step 1: Rough chop the onion.

Step 2: Place all ingredients, except the olive oil, into the work bowl of a food processor and pulse 5-6 times.

Step 3: Run the food processor and slowly drizzle the olive oil into the work bowl through the chute. Blend until sauce is mildly grainy. You are looking for a texture a little finer than oatmeal.

Chimichurri sauce is great over a steak or as a sauce on the side. It can also be played into a dozen different takes on spring rolls. It is also a license to be creative with sandwiches.

Chapter 10 – Get rambunctious with Rosemary

This herb grows into a gorgeous pine bush that is at the heart of many Italian dishes. Rosemary is native to the Mediterranean area. A member of the mint family, it is an evergreen shrub often found in association with basil and oregano.

Starting rosemary from seed is an art form best reserved for master gardeners. I have one rosemary bush that has been with me for three years now and it is the only one of 36 seed plugs that made it all the way to maturity. This is an herb that you are honestly better off buying from a garden supply nursery.

Rosemary will survive through relatively dry times and warm soil temps, choosing often to go dormant through inclement conditions rather than die. If you live in growing zone 7 or warmer rosemary will survive over the winter and come back to life like any other perennial. In fact in parts of southern Italy rosemary grows like small pine bushes.

Rosemary will also survive indoors during the winter under grow lights or in a window with southern exposure. If you choose to bring it indoors you will want to plant it in a 3 to 5 gallon planter to allow the roots to run deep. If you choose a window box rotate the planter 90 degrees every two days to reduce the effect of shading on lower branches.

Rosemary kept in the garden is a natural deterrent for deer.

Cooking with Rosemary

Rosemary is a versatile, aromatic herb used in a wide variety of dishes and ethnic cuisines. It pairs well with bread salads, soups, vegetables, meat and fish.

Rosemary really shines when paired with lamb or used as an aromatic component in artisanal breads.

Rosemary featured recipes

Grilled Rosemary Chicken

While I am very much a fan of the often forgot and sometimes maligned chicken thigh, I also recognize that the chicken breast is the most popular grilled meat in America today The most flavorful and juicy way to cook chicken breast is bone in and skin on. It also happens to be the least expensive way to buy chicken.

When it comes to grilling chicken, I can understand there are people that keep a strict eye on their calories and fat content. Since most of the fat in a piece of chicken is in the skin, this leads a lot of people to remove it. However with the skin off you're exposing the surface of the breast meat directly to high heat which will cause it to dry out.

If fat content is a concern for you, then I would advise grilling it with the skin on and removing it before plating. Some of the fat is going to render into the meat but that amount is actually rather small.

The bone is an important contributor to the flavor because the collagen in the bone and connective tissue renders out and delivers succulent gelatin into the meat.

Before we talk about the actual grilling we should discuss the marinade. My go-to method takes on an Italian flare, calling for Rosemary, garlic and lemon juice to bring out and compliment the chicken’s natural flavor.

Equipment

Small work bowl

Whisk

Large zip top bag

Charcoal or propane grill

Hickory or apple wood chips (Optional)

Probe thermometer

Ingredients

1 Chicken breast per diner

1 Teaspoon of rosemary, chopped

2 Tablespoons of lemon juice

1 clove of garlic, minced

1/2 Teaspoon smoked paprika

2 Tablespoon olive oil

Salt and fresh cracked black pepper

Procedure

Step 1: Four hours before you plan to serve, whisk together all ingredients in a small work bowl.

Step 2: Take each chicken breast and make a small separation in the membrane between the meat and skin. The hole should be just big enough for you to get a teaspoon in. The goal is to create a little pocket to hold the marinade in so it won't run off or burn away.

Step 3: Carefully spoon the marinade into the cavity. Spread it around with your finger for even distribution if need be.

Step 4: Place the chicken breasts in a zip top bag in the refrigerator and chill until 45 minutes before you plan to serve.

Step 5: Start your grill one hour before you plan to serve and bring it up to medium heat.

Step 6: Starting out you want to grill the chicken on indirect heat. Place each chicken breast just off to the side of the main heat. The breast should be bone side down with the thickest part of the meat toward the fire.

Note: This is a good time to add some wood chips to the fire if you want a smoky element. A mild wood like hickory or apple wood is the better choice over a strong wood like Mesquite.

The target temperature for the grill at this point is 250 degrees. You want to remember that you are slow roasting this chicken in order to render the gelatin and fats. If your heat is too high you risk forcing all of the juices out of it.

Step 7: After 20 minutes rotate the chicken, still bone side down, so that the thinnest part of the breast is toward the fire.

Step 8: After 10 minutes have passed, check the temperature of the meat with a probe thermometer inserted into the meat where you made the slit in the skin membrane. It should be around 155 degrees. If you want the chicken skinless, this is the time to remove it.

Step 9: Once the chicken has reached 155 degrees, in the thickest part of the meat, flip the chicken skin side down over the direct heat of the fire. Let it finish to an internal temperature of 165, which should take 3-5 minutes.

This chicken pairs well with pan roasted red potatoes and a medium red wine like Shiraz.

Rosemary Focaccia Bread

This is one of the two cherished breads of my childhood. The rich pungent flavors of focaccia bread are lifted up by the addition of rosemary. This bread is as much at home in Mediterranean cuisine as it is in down home barbecue.

Equipment

Large work bowl with cover

Plastic mixing spoon

Non-stick spray

Half sheet pan lined with parchment paper

Ingredients

3 Cups bread flour

1 Teaspoon salt

1 Teaspoon coarse ground sea salt or kosher salt (reserved)

1 Packet active dry yeast

2 Cloves of garlic, minced

2 Tablespoons fresh oregano, chopped

8 Leaves of fresh basil, chopped

2 Tablespoons fresh rosemary, chipped

2 Tablespoons fresh rosemary, chopped (reserved)

1 Teaspoon fresh cracked black pepper

4 Tablespoons olive oil

2 Table spoons olive oil (reserved)

1 1/3 cup warm water

1 Cup parmesan cheese, shredded (reserved)

Procedure

Step 1: Mix the yeast and water in a large cup. Allow the yeast to bloom for 5 minutes.

Step 2: In large work bowl, combine flour, sugar, garlic, herbs and black pepper. Do not add the salt.

Step 3: Add the yeast mix and the olive oil. Stir to combine for 2 minutes

Step 4: Wait five minutes for the water to hydrate the flour. This will help with the formation of gluten and will give the bread a proper fluffy rise.

Step 5: Once the dough has properly hydrated turn it out onto lightly floured surface for kneading.

Step 6: Lightly oil a large work bowl. (This is nice to do before you put your hands in the actual dough)

Step 7: Knead the dough by pressing it out. Sprinkle some of the salt onto one half of the dough. Then fold the other half of the dough over the salted section. Press the dough out again. Sprinkle some of the salt onto half, then fold the other half over and press it out again. Continue this process until all of the salt has been incorporated.

Step 8: Knead the dough for 5 minutes or until it will make a smooth dough ball.

Step 9: Place the dough in the oiled work bowl. Toss to coat with oil then cover.

Step 10: Leave the bowl out at room temperature for one hour or until the dough has doubled in size.

Step 11: Begin preheating oven to 425 degrees.

Step 12: Line the sheet pan with parchment paper and lightly oil with olive oil. Spread the Dough on the sheet pan gently pressing it out. Lightly oil the top and run your hands over it gently to distribute the oil.

Step 13: Allow 10 minutes for the dough to rise again and oven to preheat.

Step 14: Sprinkle the top with the parmesan, coarse ground salt and rosemary.

Step 15: Bake in the oven for 13-15 minutes or until golden brown.

Step 16: Slide the bread out of the pan using the parchment paper and allow it to cool for 10 minutes on a cutting board before slicing into squares.

The squares of bread are best torn and eaten out of hand or you can make a nice Italian Bread Dip.

Rosemary Bread Dip

4 Tablespoons of a spicy extra virgin olive oil

4 Tablespoons of quality parmesan cheese (shredded fine)

1 Teaspoon fresh chopped rosemary

1/2 Teaspoon fresh cracked black pepper

Blend with a fork until all ingredients have come together.

Chapter 11 – Seduced by Sage

This leafy herb is known best for playing well with pork and poultry.

You can start sage from seeds 6-8 weeks before the average last frost date for your region. However only one or two sage plants meet most people's needs and these days it's not hard to find established sage plants at a greenhouse supply or nursery.

If you are going to grow sage in a container it needs a planter with at least a 2 gallon soil volume in order to thrive. Since the leaves have a lot of exposed surface area the plant can dry out quickly in high heat. You should try to plant it in an area that gets good eastern sun in the morning and dappled shade in the afternoon.

Sage will survive through the winter indoors but prefers a sunny window box with daily rotation over grow lights that cause shading issues in the lower leaves.

Cooking with sage

Since sage has so much surface area in the leaves it dries out quickly and can be harvested, dried and preserved easily in late fall. Fresh sage is best for rich sauces where the essential oils can meld with the available fats and flavor compounds. Dried sage is best known for its role in Thanksgiving stuffing. Dried sage also shines in whole meat applications, such as spice rubs for roasts.

Sage Featured Recipes

Sage and gorgonzola cream sauce

You'll recognize this recipe from Part II of this book. This sauce is my wife's favorite for Gnocchi. However you could use it with just about any pasta or starch component that calls for earthy flavors. This sauce for example would go great substituted into a mushroom Alfredo.

Equipment

Medium sauce pot

Ingredients

1 Cup heavy cream

6 Ounces Gorgonzola cheese, cut into pieces

2 Tablespoons of butter

¼ Cup fresh sage leaves, chopped

2 Cloves of garlic, minced

1 Shallot, minced

1/2 Teaspoon fresh cracked black pepper

6 Baby Portobello or white button mushrooms, sliced and sautéed. (Optional)

Procedure

Step 1: In a medium sauce pot over low heat, melt the butter then sweat the garlic and shallots until they take on a little color. If you want to add optional mushrooms you should place them in the pan first and wait two minutes before adding garlic and shallots.

Step 2: Add the sage leaves and heavy cream to the pot and simmer. Stir frequently until cream is reduced in volume by half.

Step 3: Add the gorgonzola cheese in pieces. Stir until all the cheese melts and the sauce becomes smooth.

Step 4: Add the fresh cracked black pepper.

Step 5: Toss with the gnocchi or pasta of your choice.

This sauce is heavy so a white wine with brightness like a Riseling or Pinot Grigo will help cut the richness.

Sage seasoned pork shoulder roast

For most people when they think of sage, especially dry sage, they think of Thanksgiving stuffing. Sage also plays really well with many different cuts of pork.

Outside of being smoked for barbecue the humble pork shoulder roast, sometimes called a Boston Butt, is an underappreciated piece of meat. Pork shoulder is inexpensive and the leftover tend to be rather versatile. You can slice it for sandwiches, plate it with many different sides, or cut into chunks for a soup.

A bone in roast will provide more flavor because the collagen in the bone and connective tissue will render out into juicy gelatin. If you do decide to debone the roast, you should apply the sage spice rub to the surfaces the bone was cut from for additional herb flavors. Some apple wedges from a crisp apple placed into the bone cavity when roasting the next day is a nice addition.

Equipment

Shallow Roasting pan

Medium size work bowl

Large plastic bag

Ingredients

5 Pound pork shoulder roast

1/4 Cup brown sugar

2 Tablespoons smoked paprika

2 Tablespoons salt

2 Tablespoons granulated garlic

3 Tablespoons dried sage

1 Tablespoon fresh cracked black pepper

Wedges from a crisp apple, peeled (Optional)

Procedure

Applying a dry rub the night before will really enhance the flavors all through the pork shoulder roast as it allows the sage flavor to permeate the meat.

Step 1: Trim any obvious grizzle from the pork shoulder but leave at least a quarter inch of the fat cap on top. As the roast cooks this fat will render and soak down through the meat making it moist and flavorful.

Step 2: Mix brown sugar, paprika, salt, granulated garlic, pepper and sage to make a dry rub. Massage the dry rub onto the roast making sure to get it into any creases in the meat. Any extra dry rub leftover should be applied to the fat cap. Place pork in a large plastic bag, seal and refrigerate overnight.

Step 3: Bench rest the roast before cooking by removing it from refrigerator 30 minutes before roasting. Preheat oven to 400 degrees. Line a shallow roasting pan with foil and pour a quarter cup of water in the bottom.

Place pork shoulder in the prepared pan. Roast at 400 degrees for 30 minutes then turn the oven down to 300 degrees. Roast for 3 to

3 1/2 hours or until thickest part of the meat reads 180 degrees on a meat thermometer.

Step 4: Remove the roast from the oven, cover it with tinfoil and a tea towel for 15 minutes. Resting the meat like this will allow the juices to redistribute. If you were to carve the roast right away the juices would run out onto the cutting board.

Step 5: Carve off slices or whole chunks as you see fit.

This roast goes well with Butternut squash roasted in butter and brown sugar. While the dish calls for a white wine like a Pinot Grigio or a Chardonnay, you could also get away with a Pino Noir. To my mind though, this is something that goes great with a crisp, cold lager style beer.

Chapter 12 – Don't be timid about Tarragon

Tarragon is a subtle herb that plays well with earthy flavors and dishes featuring a white meat. It brings an added depth of flavor when added to the vinegar used to pickle beets.

White there are two types of tarragon you can grow, French and Russian. Russian Tarragon is known for having a bitter taste and is more useful for landscaping applications than for use in a culinary herb garden. French Tarragon is the variety that fits better with most culinary applications.

Tarragon can be started from seed or purchased at a garden supply. Unless you are absolutely crazy about tarragon you probably don't need more than one, possibly two plants. So it might just be easier to buy a plant rather than start it from seed.

Tarragon grows 2 to 3 feet in height and foliage may shade out attempts at companion planting with a low growing herbs and vegetables. Tarragon prefers well drained soil but soil that dries too hard may damage its delicate roots. As a result it prefers full sun in the morning and dappled shade in the afternoon.

Cooking with Tarragon

A lot of Tarragon's flavor comes from hydroscopic oils. This means when Tarragon is dried out it loses a lot of flavor. If you're going to use tarragon for just about anything it means that you either have to use fresh tarragon or use a method that preserves the water content of the tarragon leaves.

The two most common methods for preserving the flavor of tarragon are to freeze it when it's fresh picked or to incorporate it into vinegar, essentially pickling it. Tarragon can also be infused into oil just like rosemary or oregano.

Tarragon featured recipes

Tarragon, sautéed mushrooms

Using tarragon with beets or mushrooms is a great way to bring brightness to the dish while also accenting the powerful earthy flavors. While this dish is absolutely magical when made with wild harvested morel mushrooms, alternatives like porcini and portobello are also very good.

Equipment

Sautee pan or skillet

Ingredients

1 pound wild harvest Morels or store bought Porcini or Portobello mushrooms

1 Tablespoon grape seed oil

2 Tablespoons butter

1 Shallot, chopped fine

1 Clove of garlic, minced

2 Tablespoon fresh tarragon, chopped

2 Tablespoons chopped fresh parsley

Salt and fresh cracked pepper

Procedure

Step 1: Clean mushrooms and trim any dried part of the stem.

Step 2: Heat oil and butter in a heavy skillet over medium heat. Add mushrooms, salt and pepper. Sweat mushroom for 4-5 minutes or until the liquid is evaporating and giving off a slightly nutty aroma.

Step 3: Add shallots and sauté for 2 more minutes or until mushrooms are browned and tender.

Step 4: Add parsley and tarragon, toss to combine.

This is the perfect side dish for a steak and potatoes dinner. A dry red wine like Cabernet Sauvignon or Merlot will fit in perfectly.

Tarragon Mustard Sauce

This sauce is an excellent companion for chicken or beef. You could also use it with shell fish dishes and especially shines with pan fried shrimp. The fresh flavor of tarragon and basil plays well against the tang of the mustard and sour cream.

Equipment

Medium size work bowl

Whisk

Medium sauce pan

Ingredients

4 Tablespoons butter

1 Tablespoon AP flour

1 Cup milk

1/2 Cup sour cream

1 Tablespoon stone ground mustard

1 Tablespoon fresh tarragon, chopped

1 Tablespoon fresh basil, chopped

1 Clove of garlic, minced

1/2 Teaspoon salt

1/2 Teaspoon fresh cracked black pepper

Procedure

Step 1: Make a blonde roux by melting the butter in a medium saucepan over medium heat. Once the butter melts stir in flour and whisk for 1 to 2 minutes until the flour is light brown.

Step 2: Slowly pour in milk. Add a little bit at a time, stirring until it dissolves. Continue to cook, stirring constantly, until sauce thickens. Approximately 3-5 minutes.

Step 3: Whisk in the sour cream, mustard, tarragon, basil, minced garlic, salt and pepper.

Step 4: Once the sauce has come together you can serve hot as a sauce with the meat dish of your choice or you can refrigerate for up to two days. To reheat sauce place in a medium sauce pot on low heat for approximately 5-8 minutes.

To serve, transfer sauce to a medium saucepan. Cook over medium heat 3 to 5 minutes or until heated through, stirring occasionally. Serve warm with meat.

Chapter 13 – Tempted by Thyme

Thyme is a cousin of oregano. As such it works and plays well in sauces and soups or used to season meat.

You can start thyme from seed 8-10 weeks before the last average frost date but you should be able to source healthy young plants at most garden supply stores. Thyme can be grown as a perennial herb if you live in growing zone 7 or warmer. You can also choose to grow thyme in a container that you can bring in during the winter.

Thyme enjoys warm soil and sunny conditions as long as it is well watered. Since thyme has such small leaves it can dry out the soil in hot spells. If you don't want to water it daily during the high heat of summer it would be better to plant thyme where it gets moderate shade in the afternoon.

If you choose to grow thyme in a container you can easily bring it indoors during the winter. It does well growing under grow lights or in a window box. A purple coloration in the leaves is a sign of low phosphorus. This tends to be an issue when thyme is placed under grow lights more than sunlight. The leaves are fine to eat, simply fertilize the plant with a phosphorus rich fertilizer.

Cooking with thyme

Thyme is an herb that rarely stands alone in a dish but instead enhances the flavors of other herbs. Thyme is a little bit like a bass trumpet in a symphony, you don't always notice it's there but when it's not the music feels empty.

Thyme has small leaves that dry out easily. Whether it is used fresh or dry it easily contributes its flavor to a dish. Sprigs of thyme can be placed in a dish then removed a few minutes later after contributing its essential oils to the flavor. It can be removed from the stems and incorporated into an herb seasoning blend or spice rub.

Lemon thyme is a form of the herb that pairs well with fish.

Thyme featured recipes

Bouquet Garni

Bouquet Garni is an herb mixture used to flavor sauces, broths and soups. Traditionally it is tied up in cheesecloth and placed in the dish while it cooks. A tea ball is a good alternative if you don't have cheese cloth on hand.

Equipment

Cheese cloth or tea ball

Ingredients

4 Tablespoons fresh parsley, rough chopped

2 Sprigs of thyme

1 Dry bay leaf, crushed

2 Tablespoons fresh rosemary, lightly bruised

Procedure

Step 1: Remove the rosemary from the stems and bruise them by rolling them between your thumb and forefinger to activate the essential oils.

Step 2: Combine parsley, thyme, bay leaf and rosemary in a cheese cloth of tea ball.

Step 3: Place the bundle in a sauce or broth as it cooks. Taste periodically. Once the sauce has the level of herb flavor your prefer remove the bundle and discard.

Beef Carbonnade

This take on beef stew is traditionally cooked in an enamel coated Dutch Oven. The beer and herbs make hearty gravy that begs for fresh bread to sop it up with.

Equipment

A large Dutch oven

Ingredients

1-1/2 Pounds beef chuck roast

1/4 Cup all-purpose flour

4 Tablespoons unsalted butter or margarine

2 Medium yellow onions, chopped

4 Large garlic cloves, minced

2 Sprigs fresh thyme

1/2 Teaspoon dried thyme

2 Pounds baby red potatoes, skin on and halved

1 Quart of beef stock

1 Package of white button mushrooms, sliced

12 Ounces of dark beer

3 Tablespoons all-purpose flour

Salt and fresh cracked black pepper

Procedure

Step 1: Cut chuck roast into 1 inch cubes and dredge both sides in flour.

Step 2: Melt butter in a large Dutch oven over medium high heat. Add beef and toss until all sides are brown.

Step 3: Lower heat to medium-low and add onions, garlic, dried thyme and mushrooms. Stir often, until onions are golden. Approximately 3 minutes.

Step 4: Add potatoes, thyme sprigs and beef stock. Simmer for 25 minutes.

Step 5: Mix beer with 2 tablespoons of flour and add to the pot. Cook, stirring often, until liquid thickens. Approximately 3 to 5 minutes.

Step 6: Salt and pepper to taste.

Step 7: Remove thyme sprigs and ladle into large bowls.

This stew goes great with fresh baked bread and a full bodied red wine like cabernet sauvignon.

Conclusion

In my mind access to truly fresh herbs should be a birthright. Since I don't think they're amending the right to fresh herbs into the constitution any time soon, it means that you have to choose between buying wilted specimens at the grocery store and taking the time to grow them yourself.

I can tell you first hand that after making the upfront investment in heated potting trays, grow lights and seed pots, that the cost savings is immense.

Yes there is a learning curve involved in this process. You shouldn't expect that everything you try to grow the first year is going to thrive and yield a massive bounty of aromatic herbs. The basil might suffer sun scald, the tarragon might get beat up by hail and the thyme could dry out and die while you're on vacation.

Don't let the little failures get you down. Every season is different. Each one comes with ups, downs and lessons you learn along the way. Learn from your mistakes and each year the bounty will bloom larger than the year before. I've been doing this for decades and I learn something new every year.

On the other hand, maybe you already have a verdant green thumb but it's the kitchen that challenges you. The good news is, even if you have a long history of scorching water and burning salads while smoke detectors wake the neighbors, there is no easier time in history to learn to cook than now!

With the advent of so many cooking shows on TV and the diverse knowledge available on the internet, the answers are already at your fingertips. If you don't understand a term or a procedure in one of the recipes offered earlier, you can enter it into a search engine and insights are available.

You might be new to both the world of gardening and cooking but you're passionate to know more. If you feel intimidated, maybe you should start by making a test recipe with some of the store bought fresh herbs I was maligning earlier. Sure they don't have the magic of fresh picked herbs you grew yourself but they will get the job done.

Get your feet wet with a single recipe or two. Then maybe in the spring buy a couple of three gallon planters and a few plants at the nursery. Start small to learn the basic principles and you can decide if you want to grow from there.

A whole world of rewarding experiences is waiting for you when you grow and cook your own herbs. You just have to discover what method is right for you.

Printed in Great Britain
by Amazon

54995231R00144